GARETH EDWARDS
the autobiography

GARETH EDWARDS
The Autobiography

Gareth Edwards
with
Peter Bills

HEADLINE

First published in 1999
by HEADLINE BOOK PUBLISHING

10 9 8 7 6 5 4 3 2 1

British Library Cataloguing in Publication Data

Edwards, Gareth, 1947
    Gareth Edwards: the autobiography
    1.Edwards, Gareth, 1947-
    2.Rugby football players - Wales - Biography
    3.Rugby Union football - Anecdotes
    I.Title II.Bills, Peter
    796.3'33'092

ISBN 0 7472 2296 7

Typeset by Letterpart Ltd
Reigate, Surrey

Printed and bound in Great Britain by
Mackays of Chatham plc, Chatham, Kent

HEADLINE BOOK PUBLISHING
A division of the Hodder Headline Group
338 Euston Road
London NW1 3BH

www.headline.co.uk
www.hodderheadline.com

Contents

To Maureen, Owen and Rhys
who have been such great support
over the years.

ACKNOWLEDGEMENTS

The authors wish to thank all those who have contributed to the production process of this book. Special thanks go to Ian Marshall at Headline for his unstinting help, encouragement and advice, to Marion Paull who edited the manuscript, to Susan Dunsmore who read the proofs, to Malcolm Hamer, Gareth's agent, who did likewise and made many helpful suggestions. To all the above, and any others unintentionally omitted, our very grateful thanks.

Gareth Edwards and Peter Bills,
July 1999.

CHAPTER ONE

The Puncturing of a Passion

I can remember the exact moment I knew that Wales's love affair with rugby had died, however temporarily. It struck me with the impact of cold water on a hot day. It remains as vividly in my mind today, all these years later, as the night it happened. To be precise, it was almost six o'clock on a mild Monday evening in early September, eleven years ago. It happened on the road somewhere between Porthcawl and Taffs Well.

Taffs Well is a typical Welsh rugby village. It was the home of the famous Williams brothers, Tony, Elwyn and perhaps the most renowned of them all, Bleddyn, who earned something close to rugby immortality in his distinguished career with Cardiff, Wales and the British Lions.

It hadn't started out as a journey I would remember for the rest of my life. I was doing what thousands of dads do throughout the rugby season wherever they live in the world. I was taking my sons, Owen and Rhys, and two of their friends to play a rugby match. The chatter in the back of the car was typical of young boys filled with excitement of going to the match, or so I thought. Almost subconsciously, my mind drifted back to the times when I was their age and had travelled, flushed with a mixture of excitement and hope, to play a game. Not, of course, by car; there wasn't a comfortable saloon sitting outside our home in Gwaun-cae-Gurwen, up near the top of the Swansea valley. We travelled by local bus and never imagined any other way. But you can't blame kids today for seeing society's progress from those times, and expecting Mum and Dad to have a nice comfortable car in which to transport them to rugby, soccer or whatever other social activities they're engaged in. Times change, not always for the better, perhaps.

I wasn't even listening to the conversation that evening, preferring to concentrate on my driving. But as the traffic thinned out and we were in good time, I tuned an ear to what was being said in the back. What I heard jolted me out of any state of melancholy. The boys weren't talking about Wales, they weren't even discussing rugby. One said, 'That Dan Marino, what a quarterback. Did you see the way he won that match almost single-handed?'

'Great team, mind you,' replied another. And one of my sons started discussing in detail other players in the team.

The car all but went onto auto-pilot. Here I was, in the heart of Welsh rugby territory, with four boys going off to play in a game, and the only topic of conversation in the car was American Football, which had taken Channel 4 by storm. I could hardly believe it, and decided to investigate a little further. After all, there's nothing wrong with boys being interested in more than one sport. I could recall my own days around that age, playing countless soccer matches on our village field, imagining I was a star goalscorer for Manchester United; that is, when we weren't playing rugby.

'Boys,' I interrupted the chat behind me, 'by the way, tell me how did Bridgend do on Saturday?' It was a good question, because Bridgend against Pontypool had been the top game of the weekend rugby programme in Wales. Bridgend, one of the most powerful teams in Wales at the time, had been given a shock forty-eight hours earlier, losing by 50 points to the men from Pontypool Park. It was one of the biggest talking points of any weekend that season. It was not as though it was a question about something happening on the other side of the world; not even on the other side of Wales. Our family home is not far from Bridgend. I'd have to say they're our local team, even if the heart of the 'family elder', if I can call him that with a smile on my face, lies a little further to the east in Cardiff. Not that it mattered where we lived when that question was dropped into the conversation. Quite simply, it stopped it dead. The lads looked at each other but no one knew the answer. It had been such a startling result that it ought to have been on everyone's lips. Yet here were four young Welsh rugby-playing lads, off to a game, none of whom had any idea what had happened in the weekend matches. It turned out they didn't even know which team they were playing that evening.

I didn't ask them any more questions on that journey, but I asked plenty of myself. In no particular order, they came rushing into my mind – how is it that young lads who play rugby in Wales don't know what's going on at senior club level? What's happened to the passion for the game that almost every youngster had years ago? Why has it gone? What has taken its place? What, if anything, is needed to bring it back?

Such questions filled my mind for the remainder of the

journey. Although I'm not one for living in the past, I couldn't
help but remember what I'd been like as a kid at that age. By
Monday evenings, the scrapbook was filling up with match
reports, pictures and statistics from the big weekend games.
They'd be carefully glued in, maybe further information written
underneath, and the book carefully carried off to the bedside
table. We all had a deep knowledge of the leading points
scorers, the try scorers of the time. Facts such as those were on
everybody's lips; they dominated our everyday conversation.

In 1959, the British Lions had toured New Zealand with
some wonderfully charismatic characters in their squad, such as
Tony O'Reilly of Ireland, the English backs Peter Jackson and
Jeff Butterfield, Terry Davies, the Llanelli full-back, and Davie
Hewitt of Ireland. They didn't win the Test series but they
created a big impression, both in New Zealand and back home
in Britain and Ireland. We followed their progress avidly,
searching relentlessly for scraps of information about the tour
and latest matches.

In those days when I was growing up, it seemed as though
Welsh rugby didn't have to bother to foster a love of the game.
Generations of youngsters cut their teeth on stories of great
tries, match-winning tackles or other courageous deeds, in
village, club and international rugby. The talk was of rugby,
pure and simple. Soccer was always there too, of course, a
powerful factor with legendary players such as the Charles
brothers, John and Mel, and Ivor Allchurch; men respected
throughout their own land. But rugby was the heart and soul of
Wales. It seemed to have trademarked the one quality a sport
needs to be successful: passion. Kids didn't have to travel to
Cardiff or Bridgend, Swansea or Llanelli to see their heroes in
action; or to faraway Lansdowne Road or Twickenham. They

could see them play for their local village team each week. Dai Morris worked in the pit in our village. He would come up from the mine at lunchtime on Saturday, get cleaned up, head down to the village pub, sink a few pints and then walk to the ground for the afternoon match. Men like Dai Morris became giants in the eyes of the small boys of my time, who watched and wondered what it might be like to play for the local club. Morris was one of my heroes, even though he was a hooker. He'd stuff a couple of old paperback novels down his socks to act as shinpads, and get on with it. He was snarling and aggressive on the field, as hard as nails, but a one hundred per cent man for his village and community.

Yet here were my sons, discussing their own sporting hero. He was no local legend, wasn't even a Welshman; rather, an American Football player whom they'd never seen in the flesh and were never likely to. It was proof positive that we lived in quite another world to the one I'd known as a youngster. That realisation unleashed in my mind a whole series of questions about the consequences for rugby union, a sport I have loved throughout my life. As I thought more deeply about the causes of all this, I remembered something my brother Gethin had said years earlier. Welsh rugby was enjoying a glorious era. Triple Crowns, international championships and Grand Slam titles seemed to be the talk of our game. In 1976, Wales celebrated their seventh Grand Slam triumph, and it was the fifth time in seven years they had either won the Five Nations competition outright, or shared it. More glory was just around the corner; there would be another Grand Slam in 1978 followed by yet another international championship title the following year. But after that, virtually nothing.

Gethin pulled me up in my tracks the first time I saw him

after we'd won that 1976 Grand Slam. There we were, sitting around and chatting about the matches we'd played that season, and how already in the 1970s the British Lions, with a sizeable Welsh influence, had been to New Zealand and South Africa and won both Test series. The sun was shining in the garden of Welsh rugby. But Gethin counselled caution.

'It's all right for you and the boys now, in this team,' he said. 'It's glory all the way for Welsh rugby. But you wait. Five years down the road, I'm telling you, we are going to have a real problem in Welsh rugby. The next generation don't have the same desire for the game.'

Caught up in the excitement of the moment, I dismissed such talk.

'Duw, man, that's rubbish. Look at what's happening and how much interest there is in the game. We'll be all right. This game will never struggle in Wales,' I told him confidently.

Who was right? The worldly wise international rugby player who'd already travelled to most of the rugby-playing countries of the globe, seen the great lands of the southern hemisphere and been introduced to some of the most distinguished people associated with the game; or the schoolmaster at Cwmtawe Comprehensive, who sat back quietly and observed events while forming his own views and opinions? Gethin's words came back to haunt not just me, but Welsh rugby in general. Years later, I remember recounting this story to Ray Williams who was to become Secretary of the Welsh Rugby Union. What he said startled me.

'I pointed out these problems and put a set of proposals to the WRU [Welsh Rugby Union] recommending that we take on the responsibility of ensuring schoolboy rugby survived. But we had always been successful and the people in charge thought we always would be. Nothing was done.'

But what had Gethin seen all those years ago, what were the factors making him believe that one of the most exciting and successful eras of Welsh rugby would not just end, but be followed by years of trouble and turmoil within the game?

Let me say at the outset that of course there are people in Wales today who are every bit as passionate about the game of rugby football as ever there were. For years, they were the rocks underpinning their clubs' existence by their willingness to work on a voluntary basis in a variety of roles. Although the advent of professionalism has meant that the game has lost many loyal servants, those people are still around today. Even if they no longer give so much of their spare time to the clubs, they continue to follow their activities with considerable zeal and interest.

But, as I have said, times change and one of the reasons for the decline of Welsh rugby – one of several, which I will go on to discuss – has been the woefully poor marketing of the game in Wales. In my view, it has been poor for a whole generation, and the reason for that failure can be summed up in one word – arrogance. Those in charge of Welsh rugby were seduced by success. They drank the champagne, they went to the celebration dinners and they thought the good times would go on forever. They just assumed rugby would keep being successful of its own accord. No one stopped to think about what was needed to ensure that happened. 'This is rugby, this is Wales,' seemed to be the view. 'This is what people will always want, will always follow.' They thought that because they filled Cardiff's National Stadium for each international, that would never change. Those in authority were not thinking about major initiatives on how to sell the game, about how to build on those successful years so that hard work and investment for the future accompanied contemporary successes. They thought it would just go on whatever happened, but time has proved them wrong and sadly lacking in vision. Such failures have cost Welsh rugby dear.

While there was this inertia at the top of the game in Wales, other sports were demonstrating the complete opposite in terms of promoting and marketing their games. Today, years later, when the damage has been done and the battle for the next generation of youngsters has been fought, won and lost, it becomes clear what a great campaign American Football launched to attract so many youngsters worldwide. Not only was American Football on our TV screens regularly each week at a time of day likely to catch the interest of youngsters, it was cleverly marketed. Teams became names of global renown; glitzy products associated with the game and clubs were successfully sold to an eager audience. Magazine programmes were broadcast about the sport and it quickly created a serious following.

Those in charge of rugby were largely dismissive of other sports. 'The audience is so small it cannot threaten us,' seemed to be the view, when the WRU should have been making moves to promote its own sport. After all, it could not say it didn't have the necessary base. The WRU was in a far more advantageous position to capture the hearts and minds of the next generation than American Football because of events taking place in its own backyard. Its job was easy compared with the task of attempting to sell a game that was played thousands of miles away and with which no one in Wales had any affinity.

What those in authority in Welsh rugby failed to understand was that you have got to work to compete with other attractions. You can never rest on your laurels or past achievements.

In these days, there is intense competition for leisure time. No sport or leisure activity is safe from outside threat. Even those which seem guaranteed the continuing support of the public must work to ensure their sport remains in demand.

Lack of even basic marketing was just one factor in the decline of Welsh rugby. There were others. Principal among these was the role of teachers and the closing of those grammar and secondary modern schools in Wales from which had come so many worthy young rugby players of past years, such as Gowerton, which produced Onwllyn Brace; Cowbridge, which produced W.R. Evans of Oxford University, Bridgend, Cardiff, Wales and the 1959 British Lions; Neath, where Tony Lewis and Brian Thomas learned their rugby; Llanelli, Cardigan and Tredegar; and Gwendraeth from which that fine centre of Oxford University, Wales and the 1962 and 1966 British Lions, D.K. Jones emerged, followed later by Gareth Davies who also represented Cardiff, Wales and the Lions. Then there was Queen Elizabeth Grammar School, Carmarthen, from which Gerald Davies went on to great deeds on the rugby fields of the world.

It is impossible to overstate the value of such schools to the entire structure of Welsh rugby. Rugby was a valued part of each school's curriculum and it was taught by an array of talented, dedicated teachers. Periods were allocated to physical education, games and gymnastics, and when it was time for those lessons, the whole class had to do them. There was a drive and an emotion for the game in Wales that were paramount among everybody in those schools. Ordinary masters teaching subjects such as geography or history were rugby nuts, always ready to help the PE masters. Everyone felt a deep cultural attachment to the sport as an integral part of Welsh folklore. Also, there was regular inter-school rivalry with great competition in the close-knit communities where there existed a tremendous sense of belonging. Traditionally, Welsh boys who played rugby eagerly anticipated the day when their school would meet another strong rugby-playing school, perhaps from the next village or town. It created a strong, healthy competitive edge which enhanced the standard of the game throughout Wales.

The enthusiasm of teachers for the sport meant that often a school might have four, five or perhaps even more masters involved in helping to teach rugby skills to boys. Such numbers were vital because they ensured that there were opportunities to develop individual skills on a one-to-one basis. As well as playing competitive matches, boys could hone their skills and learn from masters who knew the game. There were, among all these things, some ingredients of success.

A kind of unofficial grapevine operated among schools. Cardiff were one of the clubs that used to hold public trials once a season. Such an event attracted young rugby players from far and wide, all hoping they might make it. Teachers would call the club secretary and say, 'I've got an outstanding boy in my school team – can he come along?' And he would go down to Cardiff for the trial and get the chance to impress. That provided another source of development for young boys in the game.

What alerted Gethin, my brother, to the potential troubles ahead were trends he noticed in school. Thirteen-year-olds were suddenly not playing the game so much, which meant that five years down the line when that group started filtering into club sides, there was not the talent coming through. Computers, for example, were proving a major counter-attraction for young boys.

There is no doubt in my mind that the teachers' strike and its aftermath, which occurred at the start of the 1980s, also had a very considerable influence upon the future of rugby football in Wales. It might seem fanciful to suggest that one event could play a vital role in all this, but it acted as a hammer blow to the game in large parts of Wales. Suddenly, teachers who had given their free time to assist in the coaching of kids, turned their back because of the general disenchantment felt after the strike. The number of teachers began to diminish and with that went the chances of continuing to produce so many talented youngsters. The opportunities for one-on-one coaching skills sessions were drastically reduced and some of those kids couldn't even get a game because there were insufficient teachers to take them. Consequently, they went off and did something else. A damaging trend had set in.

The teachers' strike lasted a few months and in that time, little school sport was played. Even before it started, PE masters had begun to experience difficulties in getting kids to play rugby on a regular basis, but the strike compounded the problem and I believe the sport lost a whole generation through that. The game should have seen this direct threat to its traditional source of players but it didn't see the problem coming. Then it was too late.

I am not laying the entire blame for the decline of Welsh rugby at the door of one group of people. Not only would that be unfair, it would be completely misleading. Plainly, a whole series of events conspired to damage the structure of the game in Wales. Certainly, the consequences became more and more obvious.

The influence of a worldwide recession in the years around 1980 which tore at the fabric of our society in Wales was another piece in this jigsaw. Small villages dotted throughout the country were often based on huge heavy industries such as steel and coal. The plentiful employment kept those local people in their own areas often for the whole of their lives. This had two important effects. Firstly, it created a great sense of belonging and pride in the village or town when it came to rugby football, the national game, and intensified the stirring rivalries that always existed. Secondly, it offered those town and village rugby teams strong men, many of whom worked in the pits or at the steel furnace. Such men provided the backbone of the clubs and, ultimately, the Welsh national team.

I have spoken to many of my former international and club playing colleagues in recent years on this subject and there is widespread agreement among us about the importance of all this. International matches were hard for all of us, backs and forwards alike, but talk to the likes of Graham Price, Bobby Windsor and Charlie Faulkner, the old Pontypool front row, and they'll tell you that they often returned from Paris, Dublin, Twickenham or Edinburgh after a Five Nations weekend to be faced with a hell of a tough local match against the side from the next valley on the Monday or Tuesday evening. These weren't easy games, mind you; anyone with a 'name', a 'reputation' was fair game for the hard nut in the next village team who might fancy flattening a Welsh international forward, and telling the story in his local pub for the next few weeks! The pace and intensity of these matches prepared you for international rugby.

It wasn't just Welsh rugby players who benefited from this kind of intensive rugby. You only have to ask former players like England's Mike Burton for their memories of playing at places like Ebbw Vale on a Tuesday night in November to realise the value of this breeding ground of top-class players. 'Burto' broke his teeth, literally I expect, at such places.

Welsh forwards have never been seven-foot giants but the national team had always had strong, tough guys at its core. With PE regularly performed in the schools and lots of labour-intensive work undertaken daily by so many rugby-playing men, Wales profited from an extensive base of players who were as hard as nails. Much has been made of the quality of some famous Welsh three-quarters down the years but in my view we were at our best when we had strong, tough forwards who could hold their own on the international field. The combination of forwards who could do that and the wily backs, footballers of true ability, was formidable.

The transition in our society's workforce from a heavy industrial base to so many technological/white collar companies, has had a profound effect on rugby football. The demise of those communities so closely allied to the heavy industries and, worse still, the unemployment that followed, leaving kids disillusioned and free to roam without direction, played a very considerable part in this story. Had the youngsters who followed so many well known rugby names from years gone by enjoyed that same feeling of team spirit and identity, a strong local community and sense of togetherness from schooldays, things might have been very different. But the social problems in Wales as a whole exacerbated the problem.

One idea that was developed to fill the vacuum created by the demise of rugby in Welsh schools was mini rugby. It came about originally because schools were no longer providing facilities for matches at all age levels. The smaller clubs in particular saw a way of attracting young rugby players of the future by drawing them to their clubs at an early age. People who give their time freely for mini rugby offer countless kids the chance to play the game, and in the main, they do a splendid job. My chief concern in watching some of these kids play is how individual and basic skills are neglected for the sake of unit skills and what I term 'organisational play'. It seems to me that the preoccupation with winning Cups has meant that these mini rugby teams are well organised, with one or two good individuals, but to the detriment of overall skills that are vital for the future.

The fact is, after many years of mini rugby, Welsh rugby had declined. Where were those footballers whom we used to produce but seemed to have disappeared? Of course, it is too late to teach a youngster of nineteen or twenty how to beat a man. You learn that, or at least you used to, almost around the time you were cutting your first teeth. I can remember watching D.K. Jones, who was a marvellous centre, playing for Llanelli, side-stepping and beating several men. Us boys who used to stand at the front of the Tanner Bank at Stradey to get a better view almost wanted to get out of the ground straightaway and go off to find a field where we could practise those skills and try to emulate the great man. In the end, we would just about be able to control our itchy feet long enough to get home and wait for the next morning. Then we'd be on the local field, working for hours at such skills to try and do the same thing. It became part of our game. It was as though it was handed down to us, and in school we would be encouraged. Our skills developed because we spent hours perfecting them, just as young pianists or violinists spend hours practising.

During school time, anytime, whenever we had the opportunity, the conversation among us was predominantly about rugby and what had happened the previous weekend. Of course, this was in the days before television influenced everyone so much.

After international match weekends or overseas Test matches, there was the excitement of seeing clips from the games at the local cinema on 'Pathe News'. Whatever the medium for finding out about games, whatever the source of our information, there was a great hunger for the sport. It was the driving force behind me and my love for rugby. The same was true of so many of my pals from those days. Even when we had to rely on street lights, long after the end of the day, we would still be trying to perfect skills by passing or kicking a tennis ball. We would hang around street corners and the conversation would almost always be the same.

'Duw, how could that Newport lot beat us Saturday then, mun?' one would say.

'Should have kicked that penalty goal, Gar,' another might chip in. Then we'd discuss the match again, in detail. The interest was endless.

Do kids do that today? Are they out on the street corners trying to come to terms with Newport's defeat by Neath the previous Saturday, or working out where the Aberavon backs went wrong against Caerphilly? I somehow doubt it. Maybe you can't expect them to. But is the truth that they are still hanging around somewhere out there, discussing Ryan Giggs's goal for Manchester United at Liverpool seventy-two hours earlier? Or Gianfranco Zola's spectacular free kick at Arsenal?

The choice of other sporting activities and hobbies now available to kids is awesome. From rugby's point of view, perhaps intimidating would be a better word. Today, kids have far greater access to all those kinds of distractions. Therefore, unless they are positively encouraged to go down to the local rugby club or stay on for an extra hour or two at school to work on rugby skills, unless they are drawn in to the sport through circumstances, they might never have the desire to participate in what we regard as a wonderful team game. Even if they do return to the game at a later age, the initial neglect of basic skills will leave them wanting at the highest level. I believe this is part and parcel of what has happened. Undeniably, there is a general lack of skill in Welsh rugby today. You can improve your skills as you grow older but you need a basic apprenticeship in the formative years to serve you in good stead later.

Another reason for Wales's decline was the loss of an increasing number of players to rugby league in the 1980s. It had a big impact in more ways than one because the guys who went were not only outstanding rugby players, but local heroes, players such as Jonathan Davies, Paul Moriarty, John Devereux, Adrian Hadley, Allan Bateman, Rowland Phillips, Scott Gibbs, Scott Quinnell, Kevin Ellis, Mark Jones and many more besides.

To lose them made a bad situation even worse. Kids eager to see the stars of our game in action on a Saturday afternoon might well have seen them, but not in a rugby union shirt and not in Wales. Teams like Widnes, Leeds and Halifax were all too often on the television on a Saturday afternoon involved in live rugby league. It was like a scar on the ailing body of Welsh rugby that just wouldn't heal. Young, budding rugby players of the future, who were still lads in Wales, saw these outstanding players going elsewhere. It was a sad, depressing sight for young and old, indeed for anyone who loved the game. Jonathan Davies was perhaps the prime example and yet, while he frequently showed his class with some exhilarating moments, I never felt he maximised his true potential as a player in union. Maybe that was due to Wales's lack of other players of his calibre at that time. He was a great player who could change the direction of a match in the wink of an eye, but somehow in watching his obvious talent, I just felt he should have attained greater heights. But if he never scaled those peaks I felt his talent should have guaranteed, then for sure rugby league made him a more complete player. He was one of the gems of their game. At a time when we lacked real performers or success he was like a bright light. When players like Bleddyn Williams, D.K. Jones, Barry John or Jonathan Davies were at their best, it was so important for kids of those eras to see their heroes turn it on. But when Jonathan went to league, he disappeared and it was a terrible loss to Wales and to the youngsters.

I make no apologies for trying to look at this situation as a whole through the eyes and minds of youngsters. To me, they matter so much because they represent our future whether you are discussing a Welsh rugby team in the years to come, a teaching academy or whatever it is. Create continuity within your system, a system that is tried and tested, and you have the basis for a successful future. Overlook the importance of such a scenario or just neglect it, and you can be certain you will have major problems lurking down the road. This is what happened to rugby in Wales.

Cardiff recognised the problem a few years ago and have tried to create close associations with schools in their area. The top players at the club go out and coach kids, trying to bring them on, making them feel part of it. We should have done it years before but I suppose better late than never.

While I was still playing, and especially after people like my brother had started to sound warning signals about the future, I thought the Welsh Rugby Union should have put in place a structure for the future development of young rugby players. Now when I look back I question myself. Should I have been more forceful and taken more interest? Could I have helped set up some kind of scheme? However, when I wrote my first autobiography in 1978, I was considered to have professionalised myself and was not allowed to play any more, be involved directly or take any active part in the game. The same applied to many other players from that era.

Under the old-style amateur rulings, taking money in any shape or form from the game, either during or even after your playing career, meant you were professionalised and unable to fulfil any official functions as part of rugby union. Even worse, just to make contact with a rugby league club was sufficient to have you thrown out of rugby union for life. Whether you eventually signed for a league club or not was immaterial. Of course, it was draconian, especially when you consider many players had given up to fifteen years service to rugby and were hounded out of the sport, told they were no longer part of it.

Some people have asked why none of us challenged this ruling in court. You have to remember that this was at a time when the power of those in control of rugby union was still considered awesome. Ordinary players didn't 'take on' the authorities. Those in charge still met in London clubs, where entry was carefully restricted and another world seemed to exist. Everything was done in a cloak and dagger way. No player I know of would have thought to challenge the authorities and their comfortable, cosy world of absolute control. It was a bit like suggesting ordinary East Germans should have taken the Stasi, that country's notorious secret service, to court for breaches of human rights in the 1970s.

I knew what it meant to write a book and I am not complaining about that. I knew the rules and what would happen. I accepted it as it was. As a TV commentator for the BBC, I was still close to the game and continued to care deeply about it. I always have had and always will have a passionate involvement in the game. And why not? It has been my life. Rugby has offered me great opportunities; I have widened my horizons and met so many outstanding people and made great friends. The game has been good to me.

Now I look back and wonder whether I should have gone and beaten down the door of the WRU and said, 'Hey, do you realise what is happening out there; we have to get together to save the situation.' But there was no encouragement for players to become involved with the WRU. I never had a single phone call suggesting a way in which I might assist. It could have been a tiny role but I would have been happy. No one in the WRU ever picked up the telephone to talk to me or even ask my advice, still less suggest an active role. I am pretty certain that few players from our era received a solitary call. When the cracks were appearing, people who might have been able to slow down the process were never consulted. A great opportunity to use that team of the 1970s, who were household names, to encourage the youngsters to go out and play was wasted.

The sort of role that might have been so valuable was the one that the New Zealand Barbarians undertook. They went to schools in various parts of the country and played against the school team. A few very influential All Blacks played for the NZ Barbarians at that time, and they would go out and have a proper match. At half-time, there would be a short clinic to show the boys how to improve their play. For the second half, the teams were mixed up, with different boys playing alongside the All Black internationals. What a way to coach! What a way to learn the game! What a marvellous opportunity for those young boys in New Zealand! Those kids would remember that for the rest of their lives. Even more importantly, it might have been the spur to sell them the game for life, to make them really want to go ahead in the sport. Why? Because youngsters are the same the world over. They are greatly influenced by their heroes.

When I think of what players like Barry John, Gerald Davies, J.P.R. Williams, Phil Bennett, J.J. Williams, John Taylor, Mervyn Davies, Derek Quinnell, Graham Price and so many others could have offered, I feel complete frustration that none of it ever happened in Wales. Trust New Zealand rugby to get it right; trust Welsh rugby to miss so glorious an opportunity. The time was perfect for it. Other sports were starting to target kids in Wales in the early 1980s, and the youngsters were, in many cases, taking easier options. Welsh rugby suddenly didn't have ready-made heroes because the national team was no longer winning. Indeed, since winning the Five Nations Championship in 1979, Wales have won only one other Championship outright in the last twenty years, in 1994, although they shared the title with France in 1988. The game in Wales was starting to go downhill so there was a huge void. By then, I think it was becoming obvious that things were not right in our game. When you discussed it with players, coaches and teachers they all said they were having a tough time in schools. The kids wanted to do other things.

Yet I strongly believe that a powerful marketing programme could have produced results. For a hundred years, kids had come out of Welsh schools ready-made rugby players in excellent condition. If this was no longer the case, you had to sell the game to them; and you'd better start doing it, as the Americans might say, pretty darn quick and damn effectively. Certainly, the authorities had ambassadors for the game in those guys I have already mentioned. They were known throughout the country as Phil, JJ or JPR. There wasn't much doubt that the youngsters would have listened to them.

As a member of that 1970s team, I can say that we would have done almost anything. All they had to do was ask us. Why didn't they? I believe they felt the structure of the game was the reason why Wales had succeeded and always would. They felt comfortable with it; it had lulled them into a false sense of security; they felt they knew all the answers. Was it fear of having their own positions undermined? Only those in office at the time know the answer. Maybe we criticised the WRU at times, but then everyone has a whinge about authorities. The greater good of the game should have been uppermost in everyone's minds.

Since the late 1970s, Wales have had a whole series of national coaches, several of whom have been perfectly well qualified for the job, and technical assistants. The national team has also had some very able rugby players and this, too, is a subject which needs some exploring. As already explained, I believe we have not had the numbers of skilful players available that we had in the past and I tend to look more accusingly in that area than to criticise individual coaches or certain players. Of course, it would be no more appropriate to blame all the Welsh players since the end of the 1970s for Welsh rugby's demise at international level than it would be to pin the entire blame for these problems on the arrival of the comprehensive system which replaced grammar schools. Besides, a comprehensive like Cwmtawe still managed to produce some very fine players such as Robert Jones and Bleddyn Bowen, which proved that the system was not completely splattered.

I would be horrified if anyone went away with the impression that the game in Wales is completely finished. Far from it, in my view. There remains a great sense of pride and interest and little incidents convince me of that, day in day out. I sometimes meet little old ladies and they whisper to me, 'Can you come back, can you play again? The boys need you.' A lovely sentiment, even if the thought creates a certain panic in my body, especially around the knees! But what it tells me is that people do still care about rugby in Wales, it still means something to them.

How else would you explain the fact that 70,000 people went to Wembley to watch Wales's 'home' games in the 1998 and 1999 Five Nations Championships? All year people had moaned about the game in Wales and what was wrong with it yet thousands of people, many of whom had probably never been before, wanted to go to see Wales play. And what of the estimated 10,000 Welsh supporters who made the long trek to Paris for Wales's Five Nations game against France in March 1999, more in hope than expectation after our two defeats in the opening Five Nations matches of last season? That heartens me greatly, so much so that I suspect the interest will continue. Sadly, perhaps not to the same degree as before among the youngsters, but still in significant numbers in terms of support. At least those who went to Paris, like myself, saw a victory for Wales which we will never forget. Then there was the magnificent win over England at Wembley, the last-ever Five Nations Championship match and the superb victory over South Africa, the match that opened the new Millennium Stadium in Cardiff. Other memorable days.

Those fine Welsh performances had people lifting their heads up proudly once more in Welsh rugby circles. As I say, they did not alleviate all the problems that had accrued down the years, as defeats in our opening matches of the 1999 Five Nations

Championship, against Scotland in Edinburgh and Ireland at Wembley, proved. But the victories over South Africa, France, England, Italy and Argentina (twice), all between March and June 1999, allowed people to feel good about a Welsh team once more.

Success helps because people follow winners. The style of play is important, too. They can forget a lot of inadequacies if they have a thrilling team to watch, and/or a successful one. But if you have been hammered, as Wales were in the 1998 Five Nations Championship game against France at Wembley, and you also have deep problems, the whole thing is magnified. For those reasons alone, to win so outstanding a game as the one in Paris just twelve months after the horror of Wembley against the French, was supremely uplifting.

Ever since I slipped into retirement from my playing days, the legacy of that team which was together for so much of the 1970s has remained in the forefront of many people's minds. One question that has often been asked of me is, 'Did we leave those who followed an impossible legacy?' My answer is an emphatic 'No.'

I do not have very much sympathy for the players who subsequently played for Wales because, in my view, if you are left a legacy, you have to match it. It's as simple as that. For a start, you should regard any legacy as a challenge for the future: how to handle it, how to manage it; perhaps, too, how to improve upon it. If, after trying your absolute best, you find you can't match it, you have the very considerable consolation of knowing that you tried your utmost and did all you could. If you did those things, you probably got quite close to matching it anyway.

The achievement of a first cap was never likely to be

sufficiently satisfying for me. The desire for a second was immediate, and the award of a fifth cap created a deep desire to reach double figures. When that was achieved, the ambition was to double it and win twenty caps, and so on. The elation I felt when, as a young boy, I witnessed Wales winning the Championship and Triple Crown in 1965, drove me on. When the Welsh team of which I was a member won the Triple Crown and Championship in 1969, I felt a huge pride. Then came the ambition to win more titles, and a Grand Slam became my ultimate target. When that happened in 1971, we set out to help Wales do it again, which they did in 1976 and 1978. Life is filled with challenges if you look for them. Behind it all, for me, there was that love of pulling on the red shirt of Wales. I cannot speak for the other players but personally that pleasure never dimmed once during all my years as an international, and I am very proud of my fifty-three caps. Those were the things that motivated me throughout my career. They helped players like myself and all the others achieve what we achieved. But no one who followed us should have looked at that and said, 'Oh, we'll never match that record.' It should never have been a millstone around their necks; rather, a motivating factor. Those who felt unable to cope with it should not have been there in the first place.

Every time the side of the 1970s went out to play in the second half of that decade, we had to live with the formid-able expectations our achievements had created, although it is only really now, when I look back, that I am fully aware of what we did achieve in those years. I make no apologies for all that we did. Why should I, why should any of us? We should be proud of it. I would say the greatest thrill for me is not to look back and count up the tally of Grand Slams,

Triple Crowns or Championship titles. Those are just statistics. No, the real pleasure is when, periodically, Irishmen, Englishmen or Scotsmen come up to me and say things like, 'You played a style of game which we were brought up on and we genuinely admired the way you played.'

What could the Welsh sides that followed us in the 1970s have done to improve on our achievements? Well, they could have beaten New Zealand for a start and they almost did in 1978 – deserved to, as well, especially after leading 12–4, and then 12–10 with just a few minutes play left. But they lost 13–12 and that single result may well have been of crucial importance to Welsh rugby in the years that followed. Had Wales won, had they beaten the mighty All Blacks, they would have achieved something as a largely new-look side that the old Welsh team had never done. It might have been a catalyst for another successful era in the game in Wales, just as I hope Wales's first ever victory over South Africa in June 1999 will prove the springboard for a glorious new era.

Even in the 1980s and 1990s, Wales still had some fine players, rugby men of real world class such as Terry Holmes and Gareth Davies, Jeff Squire, Dai Richards, Elgan Rees, Ray Gravell, Allan Martin, Rob Ackerman, Robert Norster, Ike Stephens, John Devereux, Ieuan Evans, Mike Hall, Anthony Clement, Robert Jones, Mike Griffiths, Dai Young, Scott Gibbs, Scott Quinnell, Robert Howley and others in today's team. Not too bad a list of names, that. But perhaps those fine players were not successful as a unit for very long because of the other influences to which I have already referred. It is also undeniably true that some players who have just not been good enough to wear the red jersey have done so in recent years.

The same could be true of many of the coaches Wales had in

those times. They worked hard, were by and large most diligent, well prepared and ambitious for Wales to succeed, but for a variety of reasons they could not help their teams achieve consistent success.

I remember all those years ago when I first went to Scotland as a travelling reserve for the Welsh team, I watched in silence as Gerry Lewis, our physio and baggage man, handed out a red jersey to each player. There was a silence, a kind of unspoken respect at the act. I watched this unofficial 'ceremony' taking place and I made my mind up there and then that one day, as soon as possible, I would line up to receive one of those jerseys. When it finally happened, deep beneath the old Colombes stadium in Paris in 1967, I picked up the jersey, held it lovingly in my hands and kissed the badge. I probably did that before every match I played for Wales.

In those days, it was truly special, not least because Wales might play only four or five internationals in one season. But today? Well, you tell me – what happens when you play twelve or fourteen internationals in a single season? I would like to think it means just as much as if you play only four. Those playing today must answer. For us, it was always a sense of occasion when Wales played. Does it mean as much today?

What has happened to Welsh international rugby cannot be attributed to one single factor; many have combined to create the difficulties that have dogged us for years now. It is my fervent hope that whatever the problems of the past, Welsh rugby can revive its great traditions and passions for a bright future. While we can and should learn lessons from the past, especially in the areas where we went wrong, I believe it is time to look ahead with optimism and hope, all the while retaining the belief that this game which has been for so long at the centre of Welsh culture and Welsh society will always hold a special place in the heart of all Welsh folk, men, women and youngsters. Wales and rugby go hand in hand; long may it remain so.

CHAPTER TWO

South Africa – A Thirty-Year Quandary

I have had a thirty-year love affair with southern Africa, and South Africa in particular; a thirty-year quandary, too, over that beautiful, controversial and contrasting land. At the end of three decades of reading about the place, touring it as a player, visiting as a guest and discussing the country with people from around the world, I find myself continuing to agonise over a fundamental question – 'Was I right to tour there while apartheid still existed?'

One powerful image, perhaps greater than any other I have ever seen in Wales, pricked my conscience on this tortuous subject. The sight of President Nelson Mandela being awarded the freedom of Cardiff in 1998 in a moving ceremony at Cardiff Castle, brought back to me so many memories and images of the President's homeland.

I have never met President Mandela. I was invited to Cardiff Castle for the ceremony but was away at the time. I was also due to be introduced to him in South Africa in 1998, but at the eleventh hour he was unable to attend. I, like many others, would dearly love to meet someone I regard as one of the great men of the twentieth century, an accolade which can be bestowed upon few human beings. To have been held in captivity for more than twenty-five years and then to conduct himself in the way in which he has since his release, has been remarkable. But of all the many things he has said in speeches since his release in 1990, I suppose from a British rugby player's point of view one, more than most, gave me considerable food for thought. Hearing the great man recount how listening to the 1974 British Lions winning in South Africa had given him a special thrill set me thinking deeply about my long association with his country.

I first flew south over what I came to understand was that enchanting continent of Africa back in 1967. I was a nineteen-year-old rugby-mad youngster who thought that the gods were beaming down upon him when Cardiff chose him to tour South Africa with them in May that year. I was a young lad from a Welsh mining village. I'd been at Millfield School and, just a month earlier, had won my first senior cap for Wales, against France in Paris. Now, here I was, boarding an aircraft to tour South Africa, thrilled at the prospect of playing rugby in huge stadia in a wonderful climate. Maybe lottery winners find a higher plateau of personal pleasure but I can tell you, young G.O. Edwards was pretty satisfied with his lot in life that summer!

Like most young men, I was totally naive about politics; I was also headstrong about rugby and blinkered by my desire to compete on a sporting stage. Midway through that season, I had been chosen as a travelling reserve for Wales, in Scotland, and I won my first two caps, against France and England, both in April. If I could have played soccer for Swansea plus rugby and athletics for Wales, I would have done it all at the same time. But rugby had suddenly opened up for me and led me down this path without my being fully aware of it.

When I left for that tour, I didn't even know what apartheid was. However, I would be totally dishonest if I didn't also admit that as soon as I got to South Africa I began to see signs on public benches such as 'Niet Blanke' and 'Whites Only'. That struck me right between the eyes as soon as I got off the plane in Johannesburg and it wasn't very long before I came to realise what it meant.

But then, the whole tour was a complete education for me. We were introduced to all kinds of people, enjoyed exceptional hospitality and, most importantly in our eyes, played this marvellous game in perfect conditions. What a side Cardiff had. D.K. Jones, Keri Jones, Maurice Richards (who had scored 29 tries for Cardiff that season), Phil Morgan, Billy Hullin, Ray Cheney, Tony Williams and Gerald Davies were among the backs and up front there were fine players like John O'Shea, Billy Thomas, John Hickey and Howard Norris. It was no wonder that we beat a strong Eastern Province side by something like 34–9 just after they had toppled a touring French XV, and then we only lost to the powerful Northern Transvaal in the last few minutes.

One man from that Cardiff side did not make the tour. His name was Frank Wilson and he was a dynamic wing three-quarter who scored lots of tries. He was also a lovely guy. What may have been most relevant about him in this context was that his skin was black. Cardiff had a strong tradition of fielding excellent black players. Given the proximity of the city to the docks from where there used to be a regular boat link to the West Indies, it was by no means unusual for Cardiff rugby club to play some fast, elusive backs whose families had hailed from that part of the world. After Frank Wilson, another player from a similar background represented us, Carl Smith.

Looking back now, I can remember before that tour, there were views expressed about whether Frank Wilson would be in the touring party. I didn't understand what it was all about at that time, but I can remember the discussions. Then one day, Frank announced he wasn't available. With hindsight, I am convinced that pressure was put on him to pull out. Frank was an amiable, decent man and he may well have been good enough to make the tour as a player. But the impression at the time was that he decided to save the club a lot of embarrassment by quietly withdrawing.

Off the field in South Africa, we were undoubtedly shepherded to the areas the authorities wanted us to see. The South African officials would go out of their way to tell us why apartheid was needed, why it was proper and just. We listened and wondered and I'm sure some of the older guys among us were sceptical. But for the younger players thinking almost exclusively about their rugby, there was little concern about events in this new land.

Twelve months later, I found myself back in South Africa with the 1968 British Lions and I celebrated my twenty-first birthday on that tour. Should I, by then, have been more aware of the reality of South Africa? Probably, yes. Should I have declined a Lions tour because of it? My answer to that is I would have fought a war to go anywhere as a British Lion, especially at the age of twenty. I believe that almost every other young man in a similar position would say the same.

Now, all these years later, when the awful truth of apartheid has been laid bare for inspection, the abuses of power documented and the cynical deeds committed in that era revealed, do I feel differently about going at that time? Maybe my answer should be yes. Maybe I should feel contrite about having given some sort of succour to that evil regime, but if I am totally honest I would say I am still not convinced I was wrong to go. As I say, I hadn't really thought deeply about it when I accepted the invitations to go. Now I look back, I can see that it was easy to believe the propaganda. Even then, we got the uneasy feeling that the authorities were lavishing hospitality upon us to gloss over other aspects of their land. It suited us to hear what was being said, it made us feel better.

With the benefit of thirty years' hindsight the South African issue tugs at our consciences. Who would not make a different judgement on so emotive a topic all that time later? Yet I don't want to condemn everyone and everything associated with South Africa in those days. I am the first to say I greatly enjoyed my time there and my education both on and off the rugby field was immeasurably enhanced by the experiences we shared in that land.

What certainly did make me think more about South Africa and the uneasy politics of the country was the stand taken by John Taylor, who had toured there with the 1968 Lions and been a regular playing colleague of mine for Wales since 1967. 'Bas', as JT has been known ever since he sported a bushy moustache and beard reminiscent of Basil Brush on the 1971 Lions tour, announced that he would not make himself available for Wales's international against the touring South Africans at Cardiff during their 1969–70 tour because of his political views. Four years later, he also ruled himself out of the Lions 1974 tour of South Africa for similar reasons. Some harsh statements came John's way concerning his attitude when he made himself unavailable for that Welsh Test. 'Oh, he's been up in London too long,' said some of the London Welsh flanker, perhaps conveniently ignoring the fact that the London Exiles club contributed four other players to the Welsh team against South Africa. 'He's always been a bit odd,' said others, disparagingly. 'He'll change his mind when he's come back to Wales and had a few pints of Welsh bitter,' joked others.

Once John's stand became known in 1970, I began to think more deeply about it. I don't know that you could say it jolted my conscience but it certainly made me think much more of what South Africa really meant. I felt that if people just began to appreciate what playing for Wales meant to me, they might understand what I was thinking when John was prepared to sacrifice that. He was not only sacrificing a cap, but his position in the Welsh team, maybe for a long period of time. The selectors and Unions said at the time that they respected John's stand and he would be considered for all subsequent games. Even so, the Welsh team of that era was beginning to be a little like the Liverpool soccer team in its consistency and success. You felt you didn't want to be left out because you might never get back in.

The anti-apartheid demonstrations prior to and during the South African tour of Britain and Ireland in 1969–70, which disrupted many of the matches, brought to the forefront matters concerning South Africa. Yet they really only added to the confusion of what was happening there. I was still young and eager to play rugby against anyone, and I appeared for Cardiff, Wales and the Barbarians against the sixth Springboks on that tour and, in so doing, strengthened my ties with the players of that country, many of whom were to become close friends over the next thirty years.

It boiled down to this. The overall desire to play this game we loved was too powerful. We were young men in love with the sport; the other things that appeal so strongly to the young – overseas travel, being the subject of lavish hospitality and luxurious surroundings – were an added bonus, not to be resisted. A lifetime of experiences to treasure beckoned, and marvellous people to meet.

Dawie de Villiers was one of the finest scrum-halves of his era, a player I faced on several occasions. His distinguished rugby career, which included the captaincy of South Africa, was followed by an equally distinguished political career in the service of his country. In his time, he became the number three politician in the South African government and was very much at the forefront during the transitional period, when he was right-hand man to President F.W. de Klerk. Dawie has also fulfilled the role of Ambassador to London. In subsequent years, and at the time, Dawie and I talked a lot about his country. Conversations with him furthered both my rugby and political education. Dawie possessed a wonderful rugby brain. Besides that, he had the all-round footballing qualities that were prevalent in scrum-halves in those days: the ability to break quickly, pass accurately and kick with precision. But it was his tactical acumen which made him such a superb captain. Dawie has a wonderful sense of humour and I have always enjoyed the time I have spent in his company; he has been a fine friend.

As recently as 1998, I met up with someone I had first come across on the Lions tour of South Africa and Rhodesia thirty years earlier. In the summer of '98, I found myself in Zimbabwe for the World Schools Tournament, a splendid event which brought together some outstanding young rugby players from most corners of the globe. I had first been to Rhodesia in 1968 with the Lions at a time when Rhodesia were strong Currie Cup contenders. I was sitting watching the Schools Tournament last summer when a very distinguished figure quietly walked in to a resounding welcome. Ian Smith, the former Prime Minister of Rhodesia, was smiling broadly. He was so much older and a little frail, but the warmth of his welcome, which I'd first experienced as a member of the Lions team that had won 32–6 in Salisbury, was still strong. When I went back to Rhodesia with the 1974 Lions, I was captain for the day and we won 42–6. At that time, UDI – the then Rhodesian government's Unilateral Declaration of Independence from Britain – was at its height. The British government did not want the tour to go ahead and when we ignored that advice, the British embassies were prevented from hosting official functions for us, which was a meaningless gesture. A collection of rugby players who liked nothing better than donning official gear for a stuffy cocktail party were absolutely heart-broken by this news!

Ian Smith, whose son is now a referee, capitalised on this by giving us a memorable time when we got to Rhodesia. He has always been and remains a diehard rugby fan, very knowledgeable about the game. I thoroughly enjoyed meeting him again and talking over old times and rugby, past and present.

Playing rugby in southern Africa in the late sixties and early seventies was a special experience. The atmosphere was so intimidating at times it became venomous. Playing for Cardiff at Llanelli resembled a Sunday school outing by comparison. You could hear the small black section of the crowd but only when you scored a try – they were the only ones cheering. There was a crushing intensity about every match, a passion for the game, and a burning desire always to beat us. Most of the spectators were farmers, hard men, and they came to see one thing – the Springboks or the South African provincial team beat the Lions. A lot of the supporters took the day off and got to the games around eleven in the morning. They got their *braais* (barbecues) going and filled their stomachs with food and beer. By the time kick-off arrived, they were steaming. It all added to the boorish approach. We would be pelted from the stands with narchees, a small fruit resembling tangerines. The supporters would bring sackfuls of them into the grounds, eating some and throwing the rest at visiting players. Pelting the visitors with narchees had become something of a ritual.

On the field, your opponents would try to give you the biggest belting you'd ever known. I remember in one match against the Orange Free State played at Bloemfontein on 29 June 1974, we had a ferocious battle. Every time we got a grip of the game, we seemed to be penalised and sent back seventy metres upfield by a siege-gun touch kick from the penalty taken by J.C.P. Snyman. There was a 65,000 crowd in the old stadium and as the locals sensed the Lions might be beaten, the noise became unbearable. It intensified further when Snyman kicked a penalty to give Free State the lead by 9–7. By then, we felt it was a hopeless cause, like playing on quicksand. The more we struggled, the more inevitable our demise became.

But then, in the third minute of injury time, the Free State lock forward Stoffel Botha was injured. It was obvious he was concussed but when he was finally examined and taken off, the locals sent on a replacement immediately. In those days, you needed a doctor to certify a player would be unfit to carry on before any replacement could take the field. I pointed this out to the referee and to our surprise, he waved the player off the field and told him to wait. It gave us our chance. For the first time in the match, we had an advantage in the scrums and we made it count. The pack shoved the Free State forwards back, I went to the blindside. As I was about to dive for the line, an opponent collared me but I heard a voice shout, 'Inside, Gar.' J.J. Williams had come inside me to support and when I threw the ball behind me in that direction, he was there to take the pass and score. We missed the conversion but won 11–9. There was an eerie silence around the heaving terraces which was even more intimidating than the noise had been moments earlier. The locals couldn't believe we had just squeezed home and preserved the unbeaten record which was to last throughout that famous tour.

In 1974, the South African fans experienced something that had never happened to them that century – the Lions winning the series and threatening a whitewash of their beloved Springboks. It was almost too much for them. Just to show how special that achievement was, we were still celebrating that Lions triumph twenty-five years later with a series of parties in May 1999 in Edinburgh, Cardiff, Dublin and London. We even invited Hannes Marais, captain of that South African side, to share some of the moments with us. Hannes took it in the best of spirits and it was nice to spend time with him. But I think the memory of it all made him wince, even after a quarter of a century.

By the time I went to South Africa in 1974 with the Lions, I was so much more aware of the general political situation. It could hardly have been otherwise for I encountered more and more the arrogance of the white man. When we had landed at Jan Smuts airport, Johannesburg, it seemed to me noticeable how the authorities had removed some of the more blatant examples of apartheid. Maybe they were only superficial things, such as benches with those 'Whites Only' signs printed on them, but they had toned it down a bit, probably in reaction to growing international pressures. But away from the city, I soon realised that nothing much had changed. On one occasion, we found ourselves strolling through a one-horse town, somewhere up country, when a couple of black guys ambled up to talk. They weren't threatening in any sense, but they did obviously recognise our Lions shirts or jackets. 'What are you doing here?' they said. We took it to mean what were we doing in their country, which was fair enough. It was a view. But a local white policeman had also heard it and came over. What he said appalled me. Fingering his gun, he barked at them, 'If you two don't clear off, I'll blow your brains out.' We were not under the impression that he was joking.

Then there were the bars. On the 1968 tour, we'd be in one, and perhaps a black guy would walk in. The locals would shout out, '— off.' It was horrible. I hated that. But when I went back in '77 for the World XV match that opened the new Loftus Versfeld ground in Pretoria, it was clear things were changing. We walked into a bar to find a pretty buoyant atmosphere and for a moment, I couldn't work out the difference. Then it hit me – there were black people in the bar, together with whites. There was a different atmosphere. The topic at that time was building bridges, not knocking them down.

How do I view the wider picture so many years later? Well, John Taylor was strong enough and knowledgeable enough to say that going there wouldn't be any good at all for the future. It was his view, I respected that. Others felt differently. When we went in 1974, given all the fuss which had preceded the tour and the fact that the British government had been against it and had stopped their embassies from putting on functions for us, we made a point of seeking out black people and asking them for their views. The majority said they thought we were right to tour, a few felt we should have stayed away. But what most said was, 'You give us the will to go on.' That will had increased significantly by the time we had finished our tour unbeaten, having won the Test series 3–0 with the last Test drawn. Rugby was the game of the Afrikaner which is why the black people took so much pleasure from our win. It was as if we had delivered a blow on their behalf.

How do I know that? Because Nelson Mandela subsequently made it clear that the tour worked against the Afrikaner in the long run. The Afrikaner believed he was secure in his ascendancy but we proved by thrashing his beloved Springboks that wasn't the case at all. I know one thing – the coloured people at the matches used to go berserk with excitement when we were winning. Even if it was only for a short period of time, you could tell that they felt a wonderful pleasure and change from their usual misery.

The fact that the Lions toured under duress, without the approval of their government, meant that the South Africans were conscious as a country that there was this huge debate going on in the outside world. Mandela has said that the knowledge of such a debate provided considerable encouragement to him in prison on Robben Island. South Africa did not have television until the mid-1970s, but once it arrived, the people there were bound to be more conscious of world opinion.

It would be too presumptuous of me to say that the 1974 Lions tour caused major cracks to appear in the entire system of apartheid. I don't believe any rugby tour has the power to do that. What it may have turned out to have done, perhaps in an unexpected way, was provide one more shoulder pushing against the wall of apartheid which had seemed at one time impregnable.

What became obvious as the 1970s moved into the 1980s was that every year was becoming more difficult for South Africa until total isolation arrived. Now I ask myself, if we had not gone in 1974 and had the Lions not gone back in 1980, would Mandela have been freed sooner, would an earlier changeover of power from white to black have been facilitated? In this debate covering such a highly complex subject, I am still far from clear in my own mind about the answers to some of these questions. I still wrestle with them whenever I think about South Africa, and I suspect that process may continue for years to come.

However, on those last two questions, I do feel pretty sure of a firm and conclusive answer. I don't believe Mandela would have walked free a day earlier, had we not played some rugby matches over there. What happened in South Africa was destined to occur but it was always going to be a gradual change, a chipping away at attitudes. All sorts of events influenced that process from a rugby player like John Taylor refusing to tour and creating headlines and subsequent debate by not doing so to the Basil d'Oliveira affair in cricket and the people who made their own personal protest by refusing to buy South African fruit and other goods from their local stores around the world. It was, in my view, a drip-drip effect and I am not sure what could have turned that process into a torrent that could have washed away apartheid sooner. It was as though the white South Africans, by their very nature, were a people who had to be taken right to the wire before seeing the reality of their untenable position. Direct challenges made sooner would not have made any difference, I suspect; indeed, they may only have hardened attitudes within the white community of that country.

There is an old Welsh proverb which says *dyfal donc a dyr y garreg*. It means 'Keep tapping the stone and it will finally break'. Apartheid was always going to take time to wash out of their system. In the end, world condemnation was surely the chief factor which brought it down.

As regards rugby football, only those who have visited South Africa can appreciate what the game means to the white community there. By touring in 1974 and whipping the pride of their own country, the British Lions may have provided more of an eventual service to those seeking to dismantle apartheid than they would otherwise have done by staying away. But I use the word 'may' with good reason because no one can be certain of that. Certainly, even by 1974, I sensed there was a greater accommodation of other people's viewpoints than there had been in 1968. Part of that may have been because of the knowledge that the world at large was now starting to threaten hitherto sacred events special to the whites in South Africa, like rugby tours. Perhaps they felt increasingly vulnerable. While we were there, we took whatever opportunities we had to make people aware of the outside world's concern. Remember too, that by touring in 1974, the visiting press made sure that the subject of South Africa was rarely out of the world media's headlines. The issue was being spread into the minds of people right across the globe.

Back in 1968, all people told us about Mandela, a man who has in the 1990s touched everyone with his sincerity and humanity, was that he was a terrorist and deserved to be in jail. Nothing else. To be given thirty years imprisonment for speaking his mind seemed terrible to us, but I think it's right to say that the outside world in general was nowhere near as aware of his plight back in '68 as subsequently became the case. Eventually, of course, the man's very name became a symbol for protest and rebellion against unjust imprisonment the world over. He lit a beacon for others to follow. Perhaps we should take our lead from the man himself, who spent those long, painful years in jail. Mandela did not emerge to freedom seeking retribution and vengeance; he preached reconciliation and focus on the future, rather than dragging up the past and its sometimes bitter memories. In a sporting sense, today I am thrilled to see South Africa back playing its part in world rugby, because they are such a passionate people for the game. From a personal viewpoint, I am also thrilled because my love affair with that country continues to this day. It gives me the opportunity to re-kindle friendships that have been so important to me since those days.

It gladdened me no end to go back to South Africa in 1987–8 and talk to young South African rugby men, such as the impressive Morne du Plessis, who were saying, 'Of course we have to change, there must be profound change in this country, it is the only way forward.' If I had seen definite change in 1978 and prior to the 1980 Lions tour, then by 1987 things were moving at an increasing pace. Finally, in 1990, President F.W. de Klerk signalled the dismantling of apartheid.

By the time there were trips to South Africa in 1995 for the Rugby World Cup, and two years later for the first British Lions tour there for seventeen years, so much had changed: the government, the people's freedom, a sense of optimism for the future whatever the problems of the present day, a sense of justice for all and so many other things. But in all that change, it was nice to see one thing remained the same. For someone who had enjoyed so much being a part of the 1974 Lions winning tour, it was marvellous to see the 1997 Lions go there and also win the Test series. Sometimes it's nice when things don't change!

As we welcome the South Africans to Wales for their defence of the World Cup in 1999, how should older players like myself, who were involved in that awful quandary of twenty-five and thirty years ago, reflect on our acts? Were we guilty of wrong deeds, did we betray the oppressed black man of South Africa, would our protest have helped speed up the process of reform in that country? After all those years, I am still of the opinion that we were right to go. I am glad I went for several reasons.

Firstly, it gave me the opportunity to enjoy some of the best days of my rugby life. Secondly, it gave me a far greater insight into understanding people. Thirdly, it helped me to comprehend better the whole issue of world politics. Fourthly, I made and still maintain to this day some wonderful South African friends.

Nelson Mandela has pricked, ever so subtly, everyone's conscience over South Africa. Perhaps others, such as those who knew exactly what was going on in the Republic for all those years and yet still took the opportunity for personal profit and gain, have more to reproach themselves for than a handful of young rugby players who went chasing a dream, an experience of a lifetime. We weren't paid for it, we didn't receive a penny. Others made plenty out of us and our efforts, but our consciences can be completely clear on that front.

From my personal viewpoint, South Africa has felt like a second home to me, over the last thirty years. I feel an affinity with the country, I cared about its welfare and still do. I follow its constant trials and tribulations with great interest. Today, I am concerned about its future given the uncertainty and the serious crime problem that has continued after the breakdown of apartheid.

Perhaps the final word should go to one of South African sport's greatest figures, Gary Player. He has made his worldwide name and reputation in another sport but he played rugby at school and has been a great fan of the game all his life. Indeed, before the Lions' final Test against South Africa in 1974, Gary Player's request to go into the Springboks' dressing-room was granted by the authorities. He told the players, 'I want you to go out and die for your country today. I will take care of all your families – just lay your bodies on the line for South Africa in this match.' No wonder we couldn't win that final Test!

In both years that I toured South Africa with a Lions squad, 1968 and 1974, by an extraordinary coincidence Gary Player won the British Open Championship, the great prize of the golfing world, in many people's eyes. When Player returned from Royal Lytham in '74 to his beloved South Africa, his aides made contact with the Lions squad and asked if a few of us would be prepared to go and meet him at his home and play a round of golf with him at his Killarney course, his first professional job. We jumped at the chance. Mike Gibson who was a very useful golfer, Gordon Brown of Troon, whom we assumed must be good at the game coming from a place where they stage the Open Championship, and I duly played a round with Gary. The whole day was a great experience for us. The way he conducted himself, the way he had time for everyone was a lesson to us all. Nothing was too much effort. Gary has always advocated building bridges and he was fully aware of that need all those years ago.

At the end of the round during which he passed on tips to all of us and charmed the two thousand or so local people who walked around the course watching, he took us back for dinner at his ranch outside Johannesburg. It remains a day I shall never forget, one of the real highlights of my playing days. On the golf course, Gary gave a wonderful exhibition of the control required to play the game successfully. He demonstrated how to play out of bunkers, how to chip perfectly and putt effectively. Perhaps more importantly, he knew so much about the controversy regarding colour inside and outside South Africa. He had been severely criticised by some sections of the community in his homeland for employing a black caddie during major tournaments in the United States, but he made no apologies for that.

What Gary Player said to us when we met him that day I still remember all this time later. 'I want to thank you for coming to South Africa,' he told us. Playing golf with us and offering supreme hospitality was his way of saying thanks to the Lions. He was very clear in his mind that we had done the right thing. 'This will help. You will contribute more to the breakdown of apartheid by coming than by staying at home,' he assured us.

I will never forget either his words or that day. And I'll never forget the marvellous times I have experienced in his country. It might well have caused deep uneasiness within my mind, a nagging uncertainty that has persisted for many years about whether we did the right thing in maintaining contact with a country which operated apartheid. But people like Nelson Mandela and Gary Player do not blame us for our sporting associations with their country in those years. Thus, after so much soul-searching, I cannot honestly say I find it in my heart to be critical of either myself or indeed any of us who went on those rugby tours.

CHAPTER THREE

The Northern Hemisphere – A Lost Opportunity

Dreaming about what might have been, opportunities lost or situations unexploited, has never occupied very much of my time, especially on the rugby field. You'd probably end up in the funny farm long before your career should have finished, if you tried to unravel the exact whys and wherefores of your playing career. No matter at which level you operated, all that matters is to be able to look back on it with an air of satisfaction and inner pride. No one has ever achieved all he would have wished; that is a fact of life. But fantasising about a match you might have won there, and a try you could have scored here, is all rather pointless to my way of thinking.

Nevertheless, reassessing the game from a distance of some years can be a very worthwhile exercise. When I look back over my career and the time when I played, one question looms larger than any other. Did the northern hemisphere miss a major chance to dominate the rugby-playing world, maybe for decades, when it established supremacy over the strongest countries of the southern hemisphere in the first half of the 1970s? Could Britain and Ireland have enjoyed, and retained, the kind of leadership of the game which seems to have been the unofficial preserve of the southern hemisphere nations, especially New Zealand, since the late 1970s?

Whichever way you look at it, British rugby had scaled the peak of the world game by the end of the British Lions tour of South Africa in July 1974. Not only had those Lions, led by Willie-John McBride, beaten the Springboks 3–0 in the Test series, but three years earlier, the 1971 British Lions captained by John Dawes, had upset the All Blacks 2–1 in New Zealand. There was plenty more evidence from which to construct a decent case that the northern hemisphere enjoyed supremacy in world rugby.

In 1969, England beat South Africa at Twickenham and three years later, achieved an incredible 18–9 victory over the 'Boks at Ellis Park, Johannesburg. In 1973, England went to New Zealand and beat the All Blacks 16–10 at Eden Park, Auckland. It's fair to say that result made a few people who scoffed at the poor results of the English in the annual Five Nations tournament around that time, sit up and take notice. I might add that I wasn't among those doing the scoffing. I'd seen enough quality players around the English club scene to know that this was a giant that might have been slumbering but certainly wasn't in a state of terminal sickness. Later that same year, England faced Australia at Twickenham and crushed them 20–3.

Scotland, too, had enjoyed some results to cherish against the southern hemisphere's finest in that five- or six-year period from 1969 to 1974–5. In 1969, they beat South Africa 6–3 at Murrayfield and in 1975, they beat Australia in Edinburgh. As late as 1982, the Scots were still toppling southern hemisphere nations, beating Australia 12–7 in Brisbane on a short, two-Test tour which ended in a drawn series.

To this day, Ireland have never beaten New Zealand but in 1973, they came closest to ending that unwanted record with a 10–10 draw in Dublin. In 1970, they also held South Africa, 8–8, in Dublin. In 1979, Ireland won a two-match Test series in Australia, 2–0, an outstanding achievement.

What of Wales? When I first played against the All Blacks in 1967, a game we lost 13–6, we had won more matches between the two countries than the New Zealanders. Wales fought out a 6–6 draw with South Africa in Cardiff in 1970 and as for Australia, we enjoyed a hat-trick of successes against them, winning 19–16 in Sydney in 1969, 24–0 in Cardiff in 1973 and 28–3 in Cardiff in 1975. My club, Cardiff, have never lost to Australia and have beaten New Zealand in the past.

Of course, different results in varying venues can be attributed to quite different circumstances. Nevertheless, if you put all those results together in that era from 1969–74, there is little doubt that the northern hemisphere ruled the roost. It had the power players up front and the speedy and talented backs behind the scrum to capitalise on its possession. Every major southern hemisphere nation struggled to contain the northern hemisphere's finest. The legacy of this powerful position at the summit of the world game was still in evidence in 1977 when the British Lions went back to New Zealand. So overwhelmingly superior was the Lions forward pack that the mighty All Blacks, once feared by all the world, took to putting only three forwards into their scrums during the last few Test matches. The reason for this extraordinary dollop of humble pie for a proud rugby nation was that they knew they could not handle the technical expertise and physical superiority of the Lions pack; they could not cope with the power so they preferred not to try. Some admission that, for a rugby nation that had produced giants of the game such as Colin Meads, Brian Lochore, Waka Nathan and Wilson Whineray.

So the northern hemisphere had the springboard to build on that ascendancy and keep dominating the world game into the 1980s and, perhaps, the 1990s. What happened? The British Lions won only one more Test series after 1974 – the 1989 tour of Australia – until the 1997 Lions won their series 2–1 in South Africa. This sorry saga included Phil Bennett's 1977 Lions in New Zealand, Billy Beaumont's 1980 Lions in South Africa (both 3–1 losers in the Test series), Ciaran Fitzgerald's 1983 Lions in New Zealand (whitewashed 4–0 in the Tests) and Gavin Hastings' 1993 Lions in New Zealand (2–1 Test series losers).

Even worse, the record of the three major southern hemi-sphere nations against all the individual four Home Union countries over a twenty-year period from 1978 to 1998, makes for very sobering reading. At the time of writing, New Zealand's record in Tests against England, Wales, Scotland and Ireland in that era reads: played 39, won 35, drawn 2, lost 2. South Africa's record reads: played 18, won 16, lost 2. Australia's reads: played 42, won 32, drawn 1, lost 9. This gives the southern hemisphere's three leading rugby nations a success record of 83 wins and three draws from 99 games.

I find such statistics humbling and shocking. More to the point, how, why and where did the northern hemisphere allow its dominance to slip so disastrously through its fingers?

I didn't fully appreciate what those two particular Lions tours, in 1971 and 1974, really meant until years later. We became the first British team to win a Test series in New Zealand this century and the first side to take a Test series in South Africa. The New Zealand All Blacks, for example, did not win a series in South Africa until 1996. Our achievement was recorded a full quarter of a century earlier.

Incidentally, while on the subject of Lions tours, I confess to my misgivings over the way they have changed down the years. Take the 1997 Lions in South Africa. Their schedule was such that there was no chance for them to see what we saw, or enjoy the experiences we so benefited from during our tours there. Nowadays, Lions tours have become so abbreviated. In 1968, the Lions played twenty matches on their South African tour including one in Rhodesia. In 1974, we played twenty-two games. In 1997, the Lions played thirteen games and spent little more than six weeks on tour. In 1974, we left London on 6 May and returned on 30 July, a period of just over twelve weeks. It's fair to say that in that time, we would have seen more than twice as much of the country as Martin Johnson's '97 Lions. Their visit was like a business trip, which reflects life today. There is a much more calculated approach to it all; it has become a job to do – get in, do it, and get out as quickly as possible. Is that what Lions tours should be like?

For me, seeing the country, meeting people from all backgrounds, having time off to go up country, enjoying a few days rest in the famous game reserves and generally having the opportunity to do things other than train and play, was what made such a tour so special. It became much more than a rugby tour; it was the experience of a lifetime. The chance to have a couple of days off for fishing or sight-seeing; the opportunity to enjoy a few beers together in such magical surroundings as the Kruger National Park at night, round a camp fire, with the sound of the wild animals in the game reserve . . . those were the things that made a Lions tour of South Africa unique for me. I am convinced I had the best Lions years during my career. We never received any money for reaching the level of the British Lions, the pinnacle of our playing careers. But to wear the Lions emblem on our blazers and the famous red shirt with the Lions crest, created a pride beyond price. Lions tours offered us opportunities to see the world, play the game we loved against the best teams in the world and make friendships among team-mates and opponents which would last for a lifetime. No one can put a price on such things, their benefits are beyond mere money. But today? Well, the game has changed so much. It will never be the same for any future Lions.

The '97 Lions tour became a money-making exercise, as witnessed by the 'fly-on-the-wall' documentary which was shot throughout the tour. It showed everything, nuts and bolts of the inner sanctum, the lot. Afterwards, many people came up to me and said, 'Wasn't it great, Gareth?' In my opinion, it was awful; I hated it. For me, they had betrayed that private world of seclusion which has been so special to Lions rugby men down the years. What goes on in the dressing-room should remain there, in my view. That film took a lot of the mystique not only out of the dressing-room but out of the whole Lions concept, too. To me, the powers that be behind the 1997 Lions sold their soul and that of all Lions parties. I bitterly regret that.

Of course, there were other significant differences. The travelling press troupe had become a small army by 1997. The friendship and lighthearted banter with the handful of correspondents who had been on tour with us in 1968 was impossible, long gone. That also was something to be regretted.

But I digress. Let us look more closely at the shifting power base of the game in recent years. In that context, some important questions arise. Firstly, is it a fact that British rugby is only strong as an amalgam, as the Lions? Secondly, is it true that our players come back from these tours and revert to a national approach to the game which is completely different? Therefore, do we only develop that successful pattern of play for the duration of a Lions tour?

In 1971, the Lions coach Carwyn James developed a strategy of utilising any good ball that we could lay our hands on. He did this for one very good reason – he knew we would never be dominant up front against the All Blacks and therefore utilising our possession was of paramount importance. We had some outstanding footballers in their own right with extraordinary skills and with such a high calibre of players we were able to play the game off the cuff. That was how we could produce such attractive rugby, a game which was not only exciting but successful.

This was before the days of intensive unit skills, the regimental approach which gradually came into existence as the 1970s progressed. Carwyn's idea of collective pre-match practice would often be twenty minutes of cricket slip catching, and throwing each other the ball so as to sharpen our ability to counter-attack and take passes in all situations. We would stand in a semi-circle and the ball would be flicked to us in no particular order. Carwyn also spent much time in one-to-one situations, advising and suggesting ideas to players.

It worked, and it had a dramatic effect on New Zealand rugby. Although the 1967 All Blacks had played a similar type of rugby under Charlie Saxton, New Zealand rugby generally had a reputation for success based on a forceful, dominant pack of forwards. Behind them were strong, controlling half-backs and although there may have been certain exceptions to the rule, it's fair to say that New Zealand backs were only really known for their solidity and strength. This policy had worked well enough for many years, even accepting the occasional unexpected reverse such as Wales's great 13–8 victory over them at Cardiff in 1953 and England's famous 13–0 win at Twickenham in 1936, a match that came to be known as Prince Obolensky's game.

Then, suddenly and seemingly out of nowhere, the 1971 British Lions went to New Zealand and won the Test series by playing entertaining, fast, exciting open rugby. It proved a salutary lesson for all New Zealanders and New Zealand rugby. Even before our aircraft had cleared New Zealand airspace at the start of the long trip home, the debate had begun about what should be done in the light of losing that Test series. Wisely, the New Zealanders did not try to fool themselves by suggesting that no one should lose too much sleep about a 2–1 defeat in a series. They looked behind the scoreline and saw significant lessons to learn. Within twenty-four hours of that last, drawn Test match in Auckland, many New Zealand administrators and media men were saying publicly, 'We must change, or we will be left behind.'

Not many thought they would change – people believed their type of game was too ingrained to alter – but change they did. It didn't happen overnight, nor all together. But over the last twenty years the approach of the All Blacks has been very different with much less focus given solely to the forwards. For many years now, All Black packs have understood that their priority is to produce fast, quality ball for those outside them. It was a significant shift from the way New Zealand rugby has been played for as long as seventy-five years prior to the experience they suffered in 1971.

The change involved a fundamental altering of attitudes and outlooks. More and more in recent years, we have seen New Zealand winning matches with sides scoring 20 or 30 points against them. Yet their strength used to be that they rarely made mistakes, were desperately hard to break down and scoring any points against them was always devilishly tough. If a match was to be won 6–5 or 3–0, they would win it. They were very good under pressure and rarely dropped passes. Yet here they were, after 1971, moving the ball much more, concentrating on creating and developing quality backs and being prepared to concede tries or penalties as long as they scored more than their opponents. Over the next couple of decades, they became so much more flexible in their play. It was one of the most fundamental shifts in a nation's rugby policy that we have seen this century, and it was born almost entirely out of what the 1971 Lions did against them. They said, 'These guys have shown us the way the game can be played.' So they duly unearthed and brought through more 'flair' players to perform this different style of rugby, what they called the modern game.

Gradually but steadily, the southern hemisphere has taken up this new style of play better than anyone, including the descendants of those who first unveiled the style, back in 1971. Yet those of us on that tour that was to become so influential in all parts of the world, had gone to New Zealand with few really believing we would win. That we did was due to the efforts of so many. There was a lot of flair in Wales at that time, besides the backbone of some fine Scottish, English and Irish forwards.

In 1974 it was different. South Africa believed they were stronger than they really were, but the Lions still had to overcome the traditional difficulties of a tour there – hard grounds, changes of altitude, refereeing – plus the expectation created by the Lions' success in New Zealand three years earlier.

Those two triumphs by the Lions on successive tours were not, as I have already shown, isolated wins – in this part of the world we all had our moments – but there was never any consistency. So what does that tell us? Was the ability there but not the pattern? Certainly, the southern hemisphere countries have always achieved greater consistency than we ever have. Wales or England might beat New Zealand or South Africa but then their selectors would change that successful team. Judgements like that can only be counter-productive. But we need to examine more fundamental elements in the search for the reasons why the northern hemisphere squandered so glorious an opportunity to influence the entire course of world rugby after those two Lions tours.

One reason, I believe, is that the game has never meant as much to people in this part of the world as it does in countries like New Zealand and South Africa. There, it is taken very seriously indeed. Until professionalism arrived in 1995, comparing the attitude of leading rugby players in, say, England and New Zealand, was always revealing. Some England internationals playing for clubs such as Harlequins would still be going off on skiing holidays midway through the season as recently as the late 1980s and early 1990s. Such attitudes were simply not tolerated in New Zealand and never have been. You played rugby all winter and you took it seriously. There was no room for a lax approach.

In Wales, people used to say that the players were a bunch of nutters because we were so mad keen on rugby. But when the passion for rugby and the expectation of people in our country lessened and became fragmented, that intensity was lost. They used to say defeat on the rugby field in Wales meant a day of mourning just as it did in the southern hemisphere. But when you got to New Zealand, you quickly realised that the intensity for the game there was altogether different, even compared to Wales.

In recent years, I have rarely felt that victories or defeats on the rugby fields of the northern hemisphere have ever meant that much. A good win or a heavy defeat might make everyone happy or sad for a while but nothing much changes, they don't alter the bottom line. Wales is as good an example as anywhere else – if defeat meant as much to the Welsh nowadays as it still does to New Zealanders, we would have put things right a long time ago.

There is an overwhelming desire to succeed that is central to the way of life in New Zealand and South Africa. Australia I tend to disregard to a certain extent because their strength has been comparatively recent by the standards of the other two countries. The pressure for them doesn't necessarily come from other nations beating them (unless it's England!), but from the existence and competition of other sports in their own country. Their survival depends not just on success but on how they play the game.

If I were asked what is the difference between a rugby player in the northern hemisphere and his counterpart in New Zealand or South Africa, I would answer in one word – attitude. Certainly, they are no more skilful than us, not as individuals anyway, but there is that steely edge to their game which creates an attitude among them that is superior to anything you will find on this side of the world. People have searched for reasons for the difference for a long time now, as if hoping to find that the southern hemisphere player eats three rib steaks a day or goes to the gym twice every day, so they can put it down to that. But it is not that. There is a physical and mental toughness about their upbringing, a way in which the authorities develop young players to suit their sport. Now that is being shown in the way the naivety and natural exuberance of the South Sea islanders are being harnessed to strengthen the overall New Zealand game. You have either got that approach or you haven't: you don't acquire it. It is an expectation from youth of the demands that will be made if you want to play rugby for New Zealand.

Some of us have possessed, still do, a similarly deep determination to succeed, even in this part of the world. I was playing golf recently and my wife Maureen, who was with me and saw the effort I was making, said, 'You won't let anybody beat you, will you?' I always had that determination; the more I succeeded, the more I wanted to succeed still further. I am not the only person in the British Isles with that approach, but maybe New Zealand and South Africa just have more people with it. I do believe it is a major reason for their success in rugby football.

As I say, rugby has never been the most important thing in Britain. In New Zealand, without question it is. The same is true in South Africa among the white population. Perhaps having so many other interests in life in Britain explains why so few former players become involved in rugby administration or coaching whereas in New Zealand, so many do – Brian Lochore, Alex Wyllie, Syd Going, Colin Meads, Earle Kirton, to name just a few. Those are the people who have been instrumental in making decisions that have greatly influenced their country's rugby. By comparison, there is a clear reluctance to get involved by ex-players in this part of the world.

Results and the reactions to them are revealing. You only had to be in New Zealand in 1971 and South Africa three years later to see how much genuine hurt was generated by these defeats. I am not saying people in Wales weren't upset when our national team lost by 90 points to South Africa in the summer of 1997, but for how long did they genuinely feel down? Wales conceded 70-odd points to New South Wales on a tour of Australia a few years back and there have been plenty of other major reverses. Have we become accustomed to these setbacks which at one time would have caused a near revolution in Wales and reverberated throughout the entire country? It encourages the conclusion that it doesn't matter as much to us as it does to them.

I don't think it's generally appreciated how much difference that attitude makes. Our players say, 'Well, I'm sorry, I did my best.' People reply, 'Never mind.' In a country like New Zealand they would not understand that kind of conversation. Putting it right is all that matters to them; personal feelings do not come into it. There is a ruthlessness, a constant driving force which compels them to be and go on being winners. It comes from an inner strength and perhaps, too, from a fear of failure. In New Zealand and South Africa, they set themselves standards and goals. You could say that in Britain we do the same but theirs are always far higher and that is another reason why we have consistently fallen short.

Sport throws up extraordinary competitors of this nature, but not in great abundance. Jack Nicklaus won time after time, under the severest pressures and expectations, and although every golfing nut has dissected the man's game and tried to ape him, no one can. Maybe more naturally talented golfers than Jack Nicklaus have existed but none have come anywhere near matching his record. That is because he took the talent he had and bolted on to it a fanatical desire to be successful, and keep on winning. Being triumphant once or twice and then easing off wasn't the man's style. Gary Player was, still is, exactly the same and so are the rugby players of New Zealand. They have this inner streak which forces them on to another victory, then another, then another. They never slacken their drive and determination, never lose focus. If they do, there is a major inquiry into why, which rages throughout their country for weeks and months, as was seen following the All Blacks' defeat by South Africa in the 1995 World Cup final.

Looking back over the last twenty or thirty years, I have seen that kind of collective intensity of approach in desperately few sports in Britain. There may be individuals achieving highly meritorious deeds, like Nick Faldo's back-to-back wins in the Masters golf tournament of 1989 and 1990, both achieved after nerve-racking play-offs. Ian Botham was another strong competitor who never knew when he was beaten and he could inspire those around him to great deeds. But collectively, where is the driving determination to reach the top and then have only a ruthless, utterly single-minded devotion to remaining there?

There comes a time in any sporting contest when your skills, fitness and method are not enough. You need to dig deeper, to find that steely edge when it becomes a battle of minds. The players I played alongside on those two Lions tours of the early 1970s were at the top of their sport, but they could drag out that extra ounce of effort and desire that perhaps made the difference between winning and losing. What made them even better was that they could do it on a number of occasions. For the Lions to go on doing it for twenty years was beyond the range of British rugby men.

After 1971, the game began to change in the northern hemisphere. It was ironic really because the '71 Lions had shown the world what was possible with only limited possession but a strong commitment to spreading the play as wide as possible. We took great delight not just in winning that series but in the way we did so. But then it suddenly seemed as though big became beautiful in rugby football in the British Isles. We started concentrating on good scrummaging, tight play and the need not to make any mistakes. This phase ushered in the era of the coach.

Prior to 1971, coaching in the British Isles was in its infancy. The 1968 Lions had been coached by the Irishman Ronnie Dawson but outside such tours, arrangements for coaches and coaching were fairly haphazard. The world thought it saw what a good coach could achieve when Carwyn James proved so valuable and inspirational a guiding hand behind the 1971 British Lions.

Incidentally, I think Carwyn's selection as Lions coach must be attributed in large part to Dr Doug Smith, the Lions manager. It would have been most unusual for a Lions manager *not* to see the coach he favoured duly appointed. I am not saying it was a rubber-stamp job but undoubtedly, once the manager had been appointed, his views would have been sought about the best-qualified coach. The late Doug Smith had forceful views on most things and I am sure he told the committee of the Four Home Unions Tours that he favoured Carwyn.

Unfortunately, many of those coaches who quickly followed

Carwyn as the trend for coaches gathered momentum, were nowhere near his class. Players had a lot more freedom prior to the arrival of most coaches, and Carwyn's genius was to recognise that putting thoughts and questions before players partly to seek their input for solutions was the best way to operate. Carwyn wasn't dogmatic, he invited ideas and points for discussion. He liked players to find the answers themselves whenever possible.

I have never had anything against coaches as such, but I do not believe that players can be pre-programmed, like robots, before going on to the field. Making the game and players more predictable seems to me to be a by-product of the coaching era; although that generalisation may be unfair to every coach, the point still stands. Coaches needed to get results to justify their existence. That was inevitable, the way of the world. But was it just a coincidence that from that time onwards sides became more safety conscious whereas before, enterprise had reigned to a far greater extent? 'If there is a reasonable chance of success, try it,' became 'Don't give anything away, kick for position and let your big forwards retain possession. Keep it tight.' This change in philosophy was, in my opinion, another of the major reasons why British rugby slipped from and then fell off the pedestal of world rugby on to which it had clambered in the early years of the 1970s.

No country in the northern hemisphere better illustrated this more cautious attitude than France, which, given their history of great running rugby with inventive back play, was the biggest irony of all.

In the southern French town of Béziers at the start of the 1970s, a coach named Raoul Barrière established a powerbase which was to transform not just the club game in France but the approach of the entire international team for more than a decade to come. Barrière built a fearsome pack at Béziers which was too powerful for almost all club opposition in France. Béziers won the French Championship in 1971, 1972, 1974, 1975, 1977, 1978, 1980, 1981, 1983 and 1984. Such a phenomenal run of success was far and away the most sustained and consistent in the entire history of the French club game. It was bound to influence the national team and under a certain Jacques Fouroux, it duly did.

France, like Béziers, began to select giant, intimidating forwards, men such as Gerard Cholley, Michel Palmie and Jean-François Imbernon. They had a massively solid front row, a powerful pairing at lock and a big back row. They also chose powerful three-quarters able to knock down the opposition, almost at will. This meant they crushed the life out of most opponents, so that they won Grand Slams in the Five Nations Championship in 1977 and 1981. By no means everyone in French rugby was in love with such a style; many romantics despaired at the absence of fleet-footed, gifted runners such as Maso, Villepreux, Sillieres, Lux and Bourgarel. But, as with Béziers, it proved successful and had a profound influence upon thinking concerning the game throughout the northern hemisphere. It helped, significantly I believe, to give the New Zealanders, who were making their game increasingly more expansive, a clear advantage in terms of the game they were trying to develop. That gap, once opened, has not been closed to this day.

The French trend was also becoming clear in the British game in 1974 when the British Lions went to South Africa. Who would have thought that our forward pack would be so powerful, on a tour of South Africa of all places, that I would get the ball as a scrum-half both from our put-in and from the South Africans' own 'feed'? This was the home of some of the mightiest forwards the game had ever known. For the Lions to have gained such an ascendancy in forward power was remarkable. As a result, I was always going forward. Some have criticised the 1974 Lions for not being as enterprising as their 1971 predecessors. I would put one simple statistic before those critics – the 1974 tourists in the Test series scored 10 tries to 1, the 1971 Lions scored 6 tries to their opponents' 8 in the Tests. Lacking in enterprise? I don't think that is fair.

What the difference may have been between the two Lions squads was that the '74 Lions had a forward pack which worked hard to subdue the Springbok eight. Some people felt that ought to have been the launchpad for us to run the Springboks ragged, but such a tactic would also have given the South Africans their only chance of a foothold in the Test series. If you play a high-risk game, it is inevitable you will make mistakes. The attitude of the '74 Lions reflected the changing philosophy of the game – we would eliminate any opportunity for the South Africans to get into the series in any possible way. Once that was done, we would see what could be done behind the scrum. I do not think anyone can blame us for taking that approach. First and foremost, we wanted to win. No one would have remembered us had we dominated possession but thrown away the winning of the Test series with mistakes behind the scrum. That was to be the fate of the 1977 Lions in New Zealand. In 1971, we had no choice, we had to play a fluid, more expansive game because we knew we could never achieve the kind of mastery of the All Black forwards which we enjoyed three years later in South Africa. If you do achieve that mastery, why not use it to its fullest advantage?

Having said all that, it may be true that we did become a little too cautious in 1974. On the other hand, the personnel were different, especially behind the scrum. Players who had been so influential for the Lions in New Zealand, such as Barry John, John Dawes, Mike Gibson, Gerald Davies and David Duckham, were no longer there in 1974, although Gibson did join the tour halfway through without making the Test side. Others, of course, came in and did wonderfully well, including Phil Bennett and J.J. Williams. But perhaps some of the others could not rival the high class of their 1971 predecessors.

There is no doubt that what the Lions achieved upfront in South Africa in 1974 made a powerful impression on the game back home. The disappointing trend which followed towards a forward-orientated game plan was made worse when the one man with the vision to keep British rugby at the top of the world game was all but ignored by his fellow rugby men in Britain. Carwyn James's talents were wasted. I believe that his isolation from the game in Wales was a fundamental cause of British rugby falling behind the southern hemisphere's. Even now, all these years later, that loss cannot be over-emphasised. The chance to appoint to an influential position someone who had done something no one else this century had achieved was missed. He had steered a Lions team to a series win in New Zealand. Surely we should have utilised his great experience and ability.

As if to prove the point, Carwyn did it again with Llanelli, masterminding their marvellous victory over the 1972 New Zealanders at Stradey Park. I still remember that day as clearly as though it were only yesterday. The atmosphere was one of the most incredible I have ever known at a rugby match; it will live with me forever. I was interested to see how Llanelli would perform because Cardiff were playing them on the following Saturday. There were 25,000 people inside Stradey and the atmosphere was electric. It seemed as though the whole of West Wales was there.

You sensed from a fairly early stage, given the way the game was to-ing and fro-ing, that Llanelli might do it. Roy Bergiers' charge-down reminded me of Ian 'Mighty Mouse' McLauchlan's effort for the Lions in the first Test against New Zealand at Dunedin. Llanelli had heroes all over the field, they tackled anything and everything. You could see the New Zealanders' frustration growing. You could also sense the mounting expectation of the vast crowd.

By the time the last whistle blew and all Llanelli launched itself into joyful celebrations, it was almost dark. The lights were twinkling in the houses on the hill up behind the ground. Down in the grandstand as I looked across at the heaving mass of people who had invaded the field to carry off the Llanelli lads shoulder high, I felt a great thrill at having witnessed it.

It is always difficult to describe atmosphere, whether it was that day at Llanelli, at a Premiership soccer match or at a big fight. All I can say is that it struck me at the time as being very special, and there have been precious few such occasions in the years that have followed. I personally have not experienced a more intense atmosphere than that. The only time I ever saw something to approach it was in February 1993 when Ieuan Evans scored that extraordinary kick-and-rush try against England at Cardiff, after Rory Underwood had been caught out in the English defence. Wales held on to the 10–9 lead that score gave them to win the match and the atmosphere that day was immense.

Carwyn would have been one of the most influential coaches

of his time but for one thing – he wasn't asked to coach Wales. Yet here was a man who was ahead of his time, a brilliant thinker and reader of the game. Carwyn was adept at using the experience of those players in his charge. One example is Ray McLoughlin on the 1971 Lions tour, until Ray's injury against Canterbury ended his tour prematurely. Yet when Carwyn got home to Wales, all he met once the initial hysteria had waned was a wall of difficulties and objections to his desire to coach the Welsh national side.

It is true there were a number of people who wanted to bring him in, but there were also a number in favour of Clive Rowlands who had been the very successful coach of Wales in 1971. Clive's prowess as a coach speaks for itself: a Triple Crown in 1969, a Grand Slam in 1971. In 1969, we should have had a Grand Slam but drew 8–8 with France after murdering them in Paris. I still don't know how we didn't win that game. Clive was a strong character. He was knowledgeable about the game and understood tactics. He could be quite dogmatic and if he felt we had to play a certain way, he would say so. He, too, had the knack of getting the best out of his players, although he and Carwyn were very different in their approaches. Both had good man-management qualities. Clive possessed a larger-than-life personality and with his gregarious attitude he certainly got those successful early Welsh sides playing for him.

With hindsight, a now famous remark Carwyn made in answer to a question probably cost him any chance of becoming coach of Wales. The question was put to him by a member of the media: 'Would you like to coach Wales?' Carwyn answered that yes, he would, but he would not stand for selection, they would have to approach him and ask if he would do the job.

Furthermore, he made it plain that he would do it on his terms – he said he would choose the side himself. In other words, the Big Five, as the group of national selectors was known, would have to go if Carwyn was appointed.

As soon as he said those things, I am convinced he sounded the death knell for his own chances of coaching Wales. A lot of his friends and supporters were disappointed he said what he did because they felt it would have been better for him to be appointed, and once part of the regime, try to change it from within. Many people felt he could have done that, but maybe it wasn't Carwyn's way. Certainly, it would not have been his style to kowtow to the powers that be.

It was revolting to see the stumbling blocks that were put in his way by officials who had not an ounce of his knowledge of the game. The short-sighted, small-minded members of the Welsh Rugby Union who kept him out did not only Welsh rugby but the game throughout the British Isles and northern hemisphere a disservice. They cost the game its guiding light. Even now, more than a quarter of a century later, I feel saddened and angry at how he was treated and what we lost. Carwyn James was one of the most innovative personalities Welsh rugby has ever produced. His man-management was wonderful; he had an exceptional vision of the game and the way he wanted his teams to play it. He'd proved in New Zealand he was a master tactician, a wonderfully astute reader of rugby. With Llanelli, he highlighted areas where he could attack the tourists that famous day at Stradey Park and it worked.

The whole sorry situation was made worse when Carwyn had to go off to Italy to find work, unwanted in his own country. Who was it who said 'A prophet is not without honour, save in his own country'? Had he been allowed a far wider role in British rugby in that early era of coaching, he might have influenced the whole sport and changed the approach which was to become too forward dominated, too organised and pre-conceived. After 1974, most sides put too much emphasis on scrummaging and static play and British rugby was the loser. The 1971 Lions provided an opportunity for us to set a pattern of play that would have inspired the world. It certainly inspired New Zealand. The tragedy was, while they looked forward and built a better future, British rugby stagnated.

No matter how successful Wales were until the end of the 1970s, I am left to wonder how much more successful we could have been and, perhaps far more importantly, what greater influence we might have exerted in the world game had Carwyn James been allowed to make a contribution. His track record suggested he might have been very influential indeed. His ideas would have stimulated debate worldwide, for the respect he enjoyed was universal. Through him, British rugby had a marvellous opportunity to be at the forefront of the world game, but perhaps it never knew what potential was there to exploit.

What has happened since those days, apart from the northern hemisphere trying to catch up the southern, without success? The most important influence on world rugby is no longer a rugby person, someone steeped in the game. Rupert Murdoch's money has decided the direction rugby union is to take. His organisations encourage a strong southern hemisphere base to generate demand in the expectation of high ratings. The game that has evolved is epitomised by the Super 12, which, for me, is a bit like one-day cricket. That is not to say I don't respect the modern-day player's skills, and the last thing I want to do is sound like an old player moaning that it's not the same as in his day. However, I do believe the game has lost a lot of the fundamental things which made it unique, scrummaging and contested line-outs for instance. They made it different from other sports because you needed short, squat men to prop and big men to jump at the line-outs. Such requirements gave everyone a chance to play the game. Today, such differences are becoming blurred by the changes which originated in the southern hemisphere. Many of those changes fill me with concern. The game is becoming too much like rugby league for my liking – big men all of approximately the same size rushing into each other and knocking one another down. The need for players of different sizes is being lost. There is no room to move on the modern rugby union field, a sign of the changes towards a league-type game.

The southern hemisphere, in their desire to attract new viewers to the sport, has gone a long way towards creating almost a new type of game. Now we are going down that path, I am not sure we can ever get back to where we were in terms of adhering to the basics. The game has been quietly drifting away from the original principles for too long now. Saddest of all, no one has stood up and said enough is enough. It is all a classic example of the way the southern hemisphere has stolen a march on us. The northern hemisphere is paying a high price for not taking a lead in the world game back in the 1970s when it had the opportunity, and charting a course for the future which others would have followed.

One of the wonders of those Lions tours I have mentioned was the way players from four different countries came together and learned a new common approach to the game in the course of a few weeks. A type of play that was consistent to all was developed and the players strove manfully to make it succeed. But what happened when we all came home? Was there any coming together of the national officials to retain that successful formula, that playing style, for the greater benefit of British rugby as a whole? Did people meet and discuss how to ensure the game in this part of the world went forward from that advantageous position? Not that I am aware of. We all went back to our individual countries and played each nation's traditional game once more. For example, David Duckham was one of the great players of that 1971 Lions tour in New Zealand. But when he went back into the England squad, they chose Martin Cooper, a kicking outside-half, and David never got a pass in most internationals. Yet in Wales, Duckham was so respected, indeed revered, that he was known as 'Dai'. Certainly, there was far more respect for him in Cardiff than in Cambridge. So was it any coincidence that his best rugby performances came when he wore a British Lions or Barbarians shirt?

One final reason for our failure is the fact that we were too insular in the northern hemisphere, our minds too wrapped up in one tournament, the Five Nations Championship.

The dear, beloved Five Nations has been saint and sinner in my view in terms of its influence on rugby football in Britain and Ireland. The annual contest staged in the early months of the New Year in those wonderful locations – Edinburgh, Paris, Dublin, Cardiff and London – has become one of *the* great sporting and social occasions of the year. For atmosphere, for great support, for a flavour of the only place to be there's no doubt that this unique tournament has been an outstanding success. I still feel that the Five Nations is something unique, but in recent years when it has been largely dominated by

England and France, apart from the odd season when Wales or Scotland achieved a rare triumph, it has lost its impact. The fact that it became almost a two-horse race, while not exactly devaluing it, took a little bit of bite out of it. With that in mind, I, like many others, was greatly encouraged by events in the 1999 Championship when so many upsets seemed imminent and some did indeed take place, Wales's magnificent win over France in Paris being a prime example.

I do not seek to decry an event which gave me so many wonderful moments and a lifetime of memories, but I think it's only fair to point out that surely the British game, its administrators and its followers ought to have been sufficiently mature and blessed with enough vision in terms of the world game, to put this Championship into context. It always was, and will remain, purely a northern hemisphere-based event that has a charm and appeal all its own. There is nothing wrong with that. The game, however, has moved on and it should not be regarded as the be all and end all of international rugby. In soccer terms, it would be like Manchester United or Arsenal sitting back in satisfaction at having won the domestic competition by beating the likes of Tottenham, Southampton and Newcastle and ignoring the challenge of Inter Milan, Juventus and Real Madrid waiting beyond their borders. Although still taking pride of place, the Five Nations has to be taken in the context of playing the southern hemisphere countries as well.

In rugby's Five Nations, beating England became the chief ambition of Scots and Welshmen everywhere, just as the English sought to topple the French each year. That was fine, all very competitive and healthy but it should never have been the extent of each nation's ambitions. However, I suspect that in too many cases, it was. Take England, around the time of the early 1970s. As I mentioned earlier, within the course of eighteen months, they beat New Zealand, Australia and South Africa, an extraordinary achievement. Yet all you ever heard about England was their dismal form in the Five Nations Championship. No one seemed to dwell on their triumphs against the southern hemisphere nations or plan to build on those victories. After their wins in Auckland and Johannesburg, England returned to disappointing seasons in the Five Nations and widespread criticism. Indeed, they didn't win that event from 1964 until 1980 and it was as though their highly creditable victories over all three southern hemisphere nations, were non-achievements. I found that strange.

By contrast, Wales's glorious run in the competition has been sufficiently well documented, yet where did it lead Welsh rugby? Did it propel the Welsh into leadership of the game worldwide? Did we build on those triumphs to go on and become the most feared rugby nation on earth? The sorry answer is equally well known.

There used to be an occasional flurry of activity in the northern hemisphere rugby calendar in November or December when one of the southern hemisphere powers toured here. Even then, I suspected that some regarded those matches as just the *hors d'oeuvre* before the main dish, the real meat course which would see England down at Cardiff again in January or the Scots in Paris in early spring. What mattered most, in the eyes of almost everyone, were Triple Crowns, Grand Slams, Calcutta Cups. There was far too much focus on those internal contests which meant we never looked at things in a global way.

In my opinion, the Five Nations has been the Holy Grail for far too long in this part of the world. While I don't deny it continues to have its place, I felt long ago that it enjoyed too overwhelming an influence. The game has moved on in the world, but not here, not enough anyway. Once, the Five Nations was the envy of the rugby-playing world, but no longer. The southern hemisphere has the Tri-Nations and things progress, times change. Unfortunately, we seem to have been unable to see this and treat a splendid tournament in a slightly less focused way. It is time, I suggest, to look further afield while still retaining our involvement and fascination for what will be called the Six Nations Championship from the start of the year 2000, when Italy joins in.

I hope that the ultra competitive nature of the 1999 Five Nations Championship will signal a re-birth for a more competitive future for northern hemisphere rugby, both when we play each other and when we take on southern hemisphere opposition. However, for most teams, the importance of the event has cramped any wish to pursue a freer style, to attempt a more expansive game. As recently as this decade, teams were still going out purely to stop others playing, and hoping to survive by kicking more penalty goals for the prized win. Where did that take our game when we got on to the world stage? The results have been painfully obvious to see.

No one in their right mind would seek to end a tournament that remains as popular as this one, but surely the time has come for us to look at it in a much more objective light, and judge it in the context of major matches against New Zealand, South Africa and Australia. Opposition of that nature will enable us to gauge where we really are on the world stage. Playing Ireland in Dublin, Scotland in Edinburgh or even England at Cardiff is always valuable but it cannot provide the sole marker for the strength of our rugby. The same goes for every other country participating in this event.

If you ponder all these factors, perhaps you will share my sadness at what has followed. We were too parochial in our outlook, too concerned with our own petty feuds and in-fighting to worry about leading the game worldwide. We were too shackled by poor coaching and we failed to develop enough high-quality players to succeed the likes of Mike Gibson, Barry John, David Duckham, Phil Bennett, John Dawes, Gerald Davies, Mervyn Davies, John Taylor, Fergus Slattery, Ian McLauchlan and others. Overall, we lacked the vision to merit any position of guardianship and leadership of the world game. Had the southern hemisphere waited for us to put our individual houses in order before contemplating the game worldwide, they would still be waiting. They filled that vacuum of leadership and have held the reins ever since. They made the running, they devised and pushed for a World Cup, they led the charge towards professionalism and they have played and, in some cases, almost perfected a brand of rugby which remains the envy of countries in the northern hemisphere. The rugby-playing nations of Europe have been left behind.

CHAPTER FOUR

England, the Wasted Years

One of the great rugby mysteries of my lifetime has been the almost complete failure of English rugby to exploit its potential in terms of its national side. Despite a wealth of playing talent through the years, it has not been until comparatively recent times that the England side has achieved anything very much. It has baffled me why not. Of all the rugby-playing countries in the world, England seem to have been blessed with greater resources than most. The number of clubs alone, more than 2000, would be enough to make the likes of New Zealand and Wales drool with envy.

The quality players who have graced the game in England shirts provide a long and intimidating list. Before my time, back in the 1930s, Prince Obolensky was one of the stars of the sport, followed in the 1950s by that fine centre Jeff Butterfield. Then there was that talented scrum-half Dickie Jeeps and outside-half Richard Sharp, a fabulous footballer, both of whom represented England and the Lions with distinction. In more recent times, England have had players of outstanding ability. Consider the following – Fran Cotton, Bill Beaumont, Keith Savage, John Pullin, Brian Moore, Mike Coulman, Bob Hiller, David Duckham, John Spencer, Peter Dixon, Alan Old, Mike Burton, Roger Uttley, Tony Neary, Andy Ripley, Chris Ralston, Wade Dooley, Paul Ackford, Nigel Horton, Peter Wheeler, Rory Underwood, John Carleton, Clive Woodward, Mike Slemen, Peter Winterbottom, Maurice Colclough, Rob Andrew, Dean Richards, Mike Teague, Will Carling, Martin Bayfield and Ben Clarke. That little lot does not include anyone in the 1999 England scene such as Martin Johnson, Lawrence Dallaglio, Jeremy Guscott and Jason Leonard. So I think we can dismiss straightaway the notion that England just haven't had the players to succeed.

But as rugby prepares for its fourth World Cup, what have England got to look back on? A runners-up place in the 1991 World Cup, three Grand Slams in the early 1990s when standards had sadly declined in most of the other home unions and one in 1980 when a fine team was at last drawn together successfully. That apart, you have to go back to 1957 for another Grand Slam and the intervening years have been marked by a series of failures and frustrations. By their standards, or at least the standards to which they surely aspired with so many fine players in their ranks, that must be a major disappointment. Yet of all the teams in the northern hemisphere, England are more capable of beating the southern hemisphere nations than any other.

Take the era I knew best. I saw England at close hand from 1967 to 1978. Let me tell you a story about English rugby of that period. It was on the successful 1974 British Lions tour of South Africa that I came to appreciate what a fine player Tony Neary was: a genuine, world-class open-side flank forward. The choice between Neary and Fergus Slattery for the 1974 Lions Test place must have taken longer to decide than just about any other position in the side. In the end, Fergus got in by the skin of his teeth, but Neary was desperately close and played some superb rugby on that tour. He was a major reason why the Lions won all their provincial games. The Welsh had such a respect for his ability that at one national squad training weekend a season or two later, we spent two hours discussing how we could restrict Neary and negate his danger in a forthcoming Five Nations international against England. Then, we went out on to the training field to practise some of the moves. When we got back into the changing rooms, someone came up and said, 'The England team is out, boys.' We looked at the paper and were struck dumb – Tony Neary hadn't been selected, even though he was fit. For us, that summed up English rugby at the time. So often, they just didn't seem to pick the right guys. Players of exceptional ability were left on the sidelines. The selectors appeared to have fundamental problems in selecting their team in that era.

It's true to say that Welsh rugby was very strong, particularly at international level around that time. Yet I can honestly say, looking back, that we never had an easy international match against England. Some of them may have looked that way on the scoreboard by the end of the game but they certainly weren't straightforward because England always had strong players in important positions. In almost every case, those were dogged matches you had to battle through for a win.

Furthermore, week in week out at club level, we feared the power and quality of the big English sides whenever we had to play them. Those night matches against teams like Gloucester and Coventry, Leicester and Bristol were stirring battles, great contests in which you would see a player in the opposing side and think why on earth hadn't he been tried at international level. England had the power, all right, but they seldom enjoyed the glory.

Even when they did begin to win consistently, around the start of the 1990s when Will Carling was captain, I don't feel they ever set the world alight, and suggest that more could and should have been made of their resources. Perhaps the English are more suited to forward play. Certainly, now that professionalism is here, preparation has become much more precise and this undoubtedly helps England's make-up. In the past, they have tended to be more regimented in approach which has made them a very difficult side to beat. To play that way appears to have been in their nature.

Good coaches grasp the character of the people with whom they have been asked to work. It just isn't possible to make racehorses out of dray horses. There are plenty of analogies for this in rugby. Graham Henry, the new Welsh national coach, has got Wales playing with the ball in hands, and he's right to do so because that is in our character. We talk about Gallic flair and the French do have a style, an expressive element within them which makes it easier for them to play that kind of fast, open, flowing rugby. Conversely, the French have tried in the past to play in a more stereotyped pattern, but it is not in their nature and when they return to their natural approach they are far more successful. As for Ireland, they are playing the game like they were twenty years ago and it revolves around, 'Play hard, knock them down, tackle everything, get in among them, shake it up.'

England's pattern of play always revolved around big, lumpy

forwards dominating possession and wise use of it close in. Yet, irony of all ironies, the one time a situation cried out for them to stick to that approach, during the 1991 World Cup final against Australia, they suddenly and quite without reason, took to hurling the ball down the backline and spreading the play as wide as possible. If ever a team threw away its chance of winning a World Cup, it was England that day. Had they kept the game tight, kept the ball close in and kept the Australian pack under the hammer, which clearly they were, I have not the slightest doubt England would have become world champions. Their pack was formidable and clearly had the beating of the Wallabies. Their ability to secure possession was paramount. Yet England seemed to go on to that field at Twickenham for the final with a pre-conceived game plan and they had no one out there to change it, when it was obvious to everyone the situation demanded closing up the game.

I remember saying at the time, before the start of that final, that if England were not careful, they would be caught between two stools. The match became almost like a replica of England v. Wales in 1968 when we were totally outplayed in every phase of the game, got virtually no ball at all, yet somehow managed to recover from an 11–3 deficit and snatch an 11–11 draw.

In the 1991 final, it was painfully obvious after fifteen minutes that Australia just weren't going to get the ball. Yet suddenly England started moving their possession under pressure, and Will Carling has got to take criticism, in my view, for doing that. He was the captain on the field, he should have changed the agreed game plan. I felt it typical of England's general approach to the game – regimented and very methodical. They didn't seem to have anyone who could change it all around and show them how to adopt a style that the situation required. They had never been very good at improvisation; they weren't flexible and that performance typified the problem. What was so sad from England's perspective, and maybe the northern hemisphere's in general, was the missed opportunity of winning the World Cup. That chance won't come around too often.

England had played a very successful pattern of rugby to reach the final, with strong performances to win in Paris and Edinburgh in the quarter- and semi-finals. Against Australia, they seemed to believe it was appropriate to play a game they hadn't attempted throughout the tournament. It was as though England thought they had to win the final in a certain manner. They forgot the cardinal lesson – you must win the match first.

For me, it was reminiscent of times gone by. During my time in the game, it always used to fascinate me the way England would have eight forwards, the smallest one being bigger than anyone in our pack, often dominate possession and yet still not beat us. Part of the reason was their selection, as I have said. They had a player on the wing or at centre, David Duckham, who could tear any side to shreds, and their fly-half, Alan Old, would kick the ball all afternoon. England never played the type of game Duckham excelled in, the kind played by the Lions and then the Barbarians against the 1973 All Blacks. The English played a stagnant game at that time. When Alan Old played for the 1974 Lions before he was cruelly cut down by a serious injury on the tour, he played some fantastic rugby, running and moving the ball as though he had done it all his life and never thinking about kicking. Whenever he wore an England shirt, he seemed able only to kick the ball.

Another superb player England had, or perhaps I should say never really knew they had, was Peter Dixon, who went on the

1971 British Lions tour as an uncapped player and appeared in three of the four Test matches. Dixon won only twenty-two caps over seven years, a poor return for so talented, effective and intelligent a player. He was a really good footballer, capable of playing the modern game even at that time, all those years ago.

Mike Burton was another example. He was a Gloucester prop, as tough as teak, the kind they turned out down the years at Kingsholm. 'Burto' could hold his own with the best; perhaps he might have tried to prove a point when he didn't have to, but that was Mike. He was a wonderful character and such people were part and parcel of the game. Nigel Horton of Moseley was another typically tough England forward. He must have been – the French respected him so much they made him an offer to go and work and play in Toulouse. They didn't recruit English players if they weren't extremely tough.

I will always have respect for John Spencer, the England captain and centre at the start of the 1970s who toured with us on the 1971 Lions tour, both as a man and a rugby player. Spencer had enjoyed something of a golden period with some outstanding performances in the centre with Duckham and he came out on that Lions tour with a huge reputation. A lot of people thought Duckham and Spencer would be the Lions Test centres. He played on the wing in his first match against Counties and Thames Valley and had a torrid time. The press got on his back, he lost confidence (how many times have we said that about England players over the years?) and never broke through for the rest of the tour. John Spencer could have sunk without trace given that start; it must have hurt like hell. But such was his character, he battled through it and his contribution as a tourist and as a team man was huge. All the good things about the game were epitomised by John Spencer on that trip. I still enjoy his company immensely whenever we meet.

In years gone by, county rugby was particularly strong in England, an importance attached to these games which perhaps was not merited. Surrey or Middlesex might play a County Championship quarter- or semi-final at some stage of the season and on the back of a single performance, one of those players would find himself chosen for the England team. When it came to the step up to international rugby, the weak link in the England side would invariably be the county player. The England selectors would soon realise their mistake, drop the county player and someone else would be tried. England never had a settled side.

Consistency in selection is essential for consistent success. It doesn't matter how many times you win the ball in a match, if you haven't got a settled pair of half-backs, you struggle. Certainly, you can always lift yourself for a one-off game just as England did in the early 1970s when they beat New Zealand in New Zealand, South Africa in South Africa and Australia at Twickenham, but sustained success? It never happened for England.

Take their half-backs. I lost count of the number of different England scrum-halves I came up against, but it was a fair few. The same applied to outside-halves. All manner of people were tried, retained for a while then dropped. Then the same process would happen with the next player. In one year, 1973, Steve Smith from the Sale club burst on to the England scene. He looked really impressive – good service, strong, quick hands. Here was a player, I felt, England would benefit from for years to come. I thought to myself, 'I am going to have trouble with this guy for years.' But what happened? After three caps in that first season, Smith won just two in 1974, one in 1975 as replacement (against Wales incidentally), one in 1976, one in 1977 (once more as a replacement), none in 1978 and one in 1979 (against New Zealand). It wasn't until 1980 that he played a full season in the Five Nations Championship. That year, England won the Grand Slam and Smith played a leading part. England should have been enjoying the benefits of Steve Smith throughout the 1970s. He would have given me and those who followed me plenty to think about. But he became just another wasted talent of that era in English rugby. England seemed to shoot themselves in the foot all the time over players like that.

Throughout that era, England seemed to cough and splutter. One minute you thought they had a very well-oiled machine only to see them malfunction through a lack of spark, being too set on safety-first rugby. Then when no one gave them a chance in a match, England would win. I can tell you, they put the frighteners on us enough times, but they never knew it.

Throughout much of the 1980s, it was a similar story. England failed to build on their Grand Slam success of 1980. I believe the big transformation in the English game has come about because almost all their top players are now playing in the Premiership. Since the advent of the Courage Leagues and their successor, the Allied Dunbar Premiership, England have never had a problem with selection. All their best players are with those top twelve or fourteen teams and consequently, the selectors know exactly who they are. They can watch all the best players in one competition, just like the Welsh selectors were able to do in the 1970s. Welsh club rugby enjoyed the same sort of close proximity then, which undoubtedly benefited the national selectors. The standards were high with cross-border matches against the English and hard, competitive games against Welsh opposition. Above all, the players were not spread out over hundreds of miles, playing in different competitions, as was the case in England in those days. The selectors could watch a player somewhere on a Saturday and see him perform in completely different conditions on a Wednesday night somewhere up the valleys. That undoubtedly gave Wales a significant advantage over the English.

If that was one advantage we had over England, another was in the field of confidence. As we built up momentum through our consistent victories, we gained more and more confidence; not arrogance, mind. We respected all the opposition because the competition was always tough and hard. Frankly, I can't think of a game we won easily. Equally, I can't remember going on to the field worrying about the opposition. There was, among us, a deep inner belief that we would win as long as we played as well as we could, worked as hard as ever and did not underestimate the opposition whoever they were. By contrast, we could see lack of confidence in the play of the England boys of that time. Their performances belied their ability, and a lack of confidence was the reason.

I must admit, we were glad that was the case because you quite often felt that, with the amount of ball England would win against you, they would have been very hard to beat had they really believed in themselves. What they lacked more than anything was that special performer, the player who could rise above himself on the day and seize the game by the scruff of the neck. They needed a player who was able to make so decisive a contribution on the day, who would settle the outcome.

One story explains what I mean. On 28 February 1970, Wales went to Twickenham to play England. We had not lost to England there since 1960 and they hadn't beaten us at all since

1963 at Cardiff, but having just beaten South Africa and Ireland, England had the confidence to play some outstanding rugby in the first half of the match. By half-time, they led 13–3 and looked for all the world like winning comfortably. It was a great day for me to be captaining Wales, or so I thought with grim humour at half-time. Then a very strange thing happened. Even though Barry John had cut the deficit to 13–6 with a delightful try, we still had a long way to go when, with twenty minutes remaining, I was injured and had to leave the field. It was agonising in more ways than one. As I was helped off the pitch towards the dressing-rooms, I heard a voice in the crowd say, 'Now we've got them. Now Edwards has gone we'll do it.' I suspect the England team felt the very same thing, because no sooner had I disappeared than Ray 'Chico' Hopkins, my replacement, had made a try for J.P.R. Williams. Soon after that, he scored one himself, setting our fans roaring with excitement as we closed on England's lead. That try by Chico made it 13–12 and when JPR converted, we had edged in front at 14–13. In the last moments of the match, Barry John dropped a goal to give us victory by 17 points to 13.

That summed up two key factors for me. England, I believe, relaxed mentally when they saw me going off. They made the mistake of not putting it out of their minds and continuing to build on what they had achieved in the first half, regardless of who was facing them. And, as I have said, someone from somewhere would always come to the assistance of Wales when we needed help most. If it wasn't Barry it was JPR, if it wasn't Mervyn Davies it would be another of the forwards. Always someone would come up trumps.

Keith Jarrett was another who did it for us against England. Back in 1967, he scored 19 points on an astonishing debut. It equalled the individual points scoring record for Wales which had been set back in 1910. Jarrett scored a try, converted all five tries Wales scored that day in their 34–21 win (England scored three tries themselves) and also kicked two penalty goals. It was one of the most audacious debut displays there can ever have been.

There have been many others down the years, including J.P.R. Williams and Maurice Richards, who have had that little bit extra that made all the difference. I don't think England ever had those players. Plenty of their guys had their magic moments but when the real crunch games came along, they just couldn't quite do it. I don't think that has changed. The young England full-back Matt Perry looks a good player but you couldn't say he is a natural runner in the class or style of the Frenchman Emile N'Tamack. Jonny Wilkinson, another young English back, is not in the same mould as Thomas Castaignede. Had Castaignede been an Englishman, I wonder just how many games he would have played for his country. I suspect he may have been seen as too much of a maverick figure. He would not have suited the English pattern, just as Stuart Barnes didn't. England chose the pragmatic Rob Andrew as their fly-half in preference to the more erratic Barnes, except on the rare occasion.

England may not have within their ranks players with the style of French three-quarters or the handling ability of Welsh half-backs, but you feel they have so much control and power up front that they could play any game they wanted to. When the standards in the Five Nations declined so dramatically, there was only one other team able to stand up to England in the 1990s – France. They alone offered that strong England side a serious challenge in those lean years for the Championship.

Stretching the limbs on the training ground in Australia in 1969 in an All Black jersey (*Popperfoto*).

Great Partners
(ABOVE) Spinning a pass out to Barry John in 1969, and (BELOW) with Phil Bennett in close support in 1974 – these two were to play outside me for virtually the whole of my international career (*Colorsport*).

The Beginning and the End
(ABOVE) John Dawes passes to Tom David at the beginning of the move in the 1973 Barbarians v All Blacks game which resulted in my famous try. At this stage I'm still catching up (*Colorsport*). (BELOW) Finishing off a move with a try against South Africa at Cardiff in 1970 (*Sport & General*).

This Sporting Life

Alongside Gary Player, one of golf's all-time legends, during the 1974 Lions tour of South Africa, with Gordon Brown (*left*) and Mike Gibson (*right*).

Fishing has always been one of my favourite sports – and now I even get involved in the politics, too.

Tennis with JPR in Tokyo 1975.

Shooting with Jack Charlton, Steve Coppell and Derek Bell in 1986 at the North Wales shooting school. My career in rugby opened up so many other wonderful opportunities.

A super scrum-half England never seemed to realise they had: Steve Smith (*Popperfoto*).

Naas Botha of South Africa, one of the great world fly-halves of the last twenty years, and, so the joke ran, one of the least likely to use his centres (*Popperfoto*).

JPR, who was and remains competitive right down to his cotton socks (*Popperfoto*).

Just getting the ball away in time in my final international, in 1978 against France, which completed another Grand Slam (*Colorsport*).

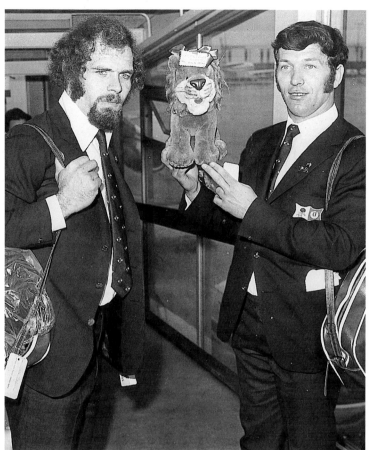

John Taylor (*left*) and John Dawes depart for the 1971 Lions tour to New Zealand (*Popperfoto*).

The welcome home after that victorious Lions tour was incredible compared to the one that greeted us in 1968.

BUW 780

I am anxious not to give the impression that everything that occurred in our era was sublime, whereas in recent years the rugby has become plodding and stagnant. That is not altogether true, nor is the claim by some that the modern players offer little in terms of skills. For example, I greatly respect Rob Andrew's ability to play the English game. He has never really had the credit he deserves. In my view, he has been quite outstanding for England down the years. You could see why a player like Barnes was wanted by some English people in preference to Rob, but the selectors decided otherwise. The trouble was, England found they couldn't dominate the world with Rob's style of play because it was too limited.

As far as it went, it was superbly executed, but it never offered enough to stretch and defeat the great sides of world rugby, the likes of New Zealand in the 1995 World Cup semi-final. As soon as a side achieved anything remotely resembling parity up front, they had the beating of England behind the scrum. Most of the good sides had jewels that could unlock defences and while I don't suggest England didn't have similar potential in players like Jeremy Guscott, they never unleashed them so that they could perform when it really mattered. The 1991 World Cup final and the 1995 World Cup semi-final are two cases in point. Perhaps those players would say they had a desire to play a wider game, but you have to say on the evidence that they only prodded at it, no more.

The Tri-Nations, the tournament which is the cream of southern hemisphere rugby nowadays, produces great team performances, but outstanding individual performances, too. In England, the system operates against players thinking as individuals. They certainly don't seem able to do it time after time. In the years from 1971 to 1973, the Welsh team had one set move for the backs with two permutations, nothing else. We knew we had to make decisions on the park relating to the game as it stood at any particular moment.

When I think what a player England have had in Jeremy Guscott for ten years, I believe they should have been opening up opponents in every game. Yet even in recent times when the standards of the Celtic nations have declined, how many times have England had to rely on goal-kicking to get the victories they should have achieved with great style and swagger? Guscott's genius, his ability to destroy defences, has been seen only intermittently, little gems which remain in the memory as special moments.

There are two ways of looking at that. You can say that it has been the player's own fault. He should have ensured he became more involved by not waiting for the ball to come to him but going looking for it; or you can say that those inside him did not release him as he and England would perhaps have hoped. Guscott and Carling played together many times, but you had the feeling that the partnership rarely hit the heights of which it ought to have been capable. It's hard to apportion exact blame for that situation but let me say this – had a team like France, New Zealand or South Africa possessed a player of Jeremy's class, I am certain a way would have been found to get the best out of him. England, sadly for them, largely failed to do that, and they were the biggest losers.

The organisation of teams is much better today than ever it was in my time. One reason we could play like we did was because we had learned individual skills, played a lot of games on our own and got used to making our own decisions and assessing situations. Rugby has always revolved around making the right decision at the right time on the field. No amount of coaching can produce that ability if it isn't already there within a player. There must be room for the individual in the game because if there isn't, it will die. The game must always have players who can make you leap up from your seat, players who can indulge in the unorthodox, do the unpredictable with glorious results. I believe this may be the answer to England's problems.

England's performances in winning those Grand Slams in the 1990s were fantastic. They completely and utterly destroyed the opposition and those triumphs were thoroughly well deserved. How do I feel former Welsh sides would have done against such a powerful team? Well, perhaps we wouldn't have got our hands on the ball; but in any game, each side gets some chances.

We have seen very efficient England sides in recent years but, quite honestly, they have left me cold. When England take over a match, as they did against Wales at Twickenham in 1998, it is clinical and highly efficient. On that occasion, they got the knife out and cut us to pieces. As painful as that was for a Welshman to watch, I cannot say at any stage I was excited by the rugby they played.

Working in television for so long has made me very objective. When France beat us 51–0 at Wembley in the final game of the 1998 Five Nations, as much as the damage being inflicted upon Wales hurt, it warmed my heart, it excited me to see such magnificent, flowing rugby, even if it was from France. Have England ever really excited people? Probably over the last twenty years there have been a few performances to make you think 'Hang on, this could be a great England side.' But it was never maintained, which is a pity for them, and for us, as onlookers.

On reflection, what made our era so outstanding for Wales was that we stamped a way of playing on the game. When it comes to winning Grand Slams, England's record is better than Wales's, but frankly, I don't care. The most satisfying thing for me today is the number of people who come up to me even now, more than twenty years after I retired from international rugby, and say how much they enjoyed the way we played the game or the way the teams of that era performed. You can tell it had a strong impact on the way they approached the game, and their expectations of the way the game should be played. Our philosophy was, 'If it's good ball, let's have it.' Simple as that. The French team of the 1960s and start of the 1970s played like it, too, just as they have in recent years under the influence of Pierre Villepreux and Jean-Claude Skrela. France's 1998 Grand Slam was made special by their style of play. It was a statement about the way they believed rugby should be performed.

England, for all their success, have had little or no impact on the way the game is developing. Undeniably, England have made themselves difficult to beat and there are all sorts of reasons for that. They are well organised and well prepared. The players are part of a highly competitive league and used to playing at the highest level. A tough club match in Wales used to generate the sort of passion and commitment that was not that far short of an international match; and England now possess an ideal launchpad for international rugby from their club base, especially when they play in Europe against French teams.

The modern game suits England because their players are so

big and it has become a big man's sport. They have the basic ingredients but it is how they exploit that potential that counts. That remains as key an ingredient in the game today as when I played.

CHAPTER FIVE

What Made That Era so Special?

The video machine in my mind's eye goes into overdrive when the conversation comes round to our era. There's Barry John side-stepping delicately through the English defence at Cardiff, like someone trying to avoid daffodils in the park; Maurice Richards's strong running taking him to the try-line four times in a 30–9 win over England, also at Cardiff, in 1969; Gerald Davies sprinting around the Scottish cover at Murrayfield for that last-minute try which brought Wales to within a point of Scotland in 1971, followed by John Taylor's perfectly calm demeanour as he coolly slotted the conversion from a wide angle, to snatch the game, 19–18. And what of Graham Price's extraordinary try after a 75-yard run against France in Paris in 1975 or J.P.R. Williams's rock-like defence the following season at Cardiff when he hurled the French wing Jean-François Gourdon into touch with a shuddering shoulder challenge near the end to secure our Grand Slam?

Such thrilling memories capture the rugby spirit of the time.

It was not just Wales who played some superb rugby. In 1970, France scored six tries to thrash England 35–13 at Stade Colombes and two years later when England went back to the same ground, they were out-scored six tries to one, in a 37–12 defeat. At that time, it was France's record score in a Championship match and also the highest score ever by any country against England. In both games, the pace, movement and free-flowing rugby played by the French sides were exceptional.

I have thought about that glorious era for rugby many times in recent years. There seemed to be a style, a panache about much of the play, and the players, which took the game on to another level, a higher plateau. There were several reasons for this.

Rugby had cast off the pall of gloom under which it had operated for much of the 1960s. Too many games had become static affairs, contests involving little more than a battle between the two sets of forwards, with the backs sometimes just bystanders. The game had seemed fragmented, slow and occasionally predictable.

Changing one or two crucial laws of the game towards the end of the 1960s had a profound effect upon the sport. Whereas in one Scotland–Wales game of the early 1960s, there had been the ridiculous total of 111 line-outs because players could kick into touch from any part of the field, the new law which decreed only those inside their own 25 could kick directly into touch, changed the game fundamentally and very much for the better. Suddenly, minds were put to generating ideas of a creative nature, rather than concentrating on safety-first tactics based around the kick to touch. Once the possibility of getting rid of the ball from play whenever danger threatened was ended, players realised a more offensive, as opposed to defensive, approach was worth pursuing. It opened up the whole game and led to a great deal of the open, running rugby which characterised much of the 1970s.

The recognition of coaches and coaching in the late 1960s undoubtedly revolutionised the game for the better. I know I have already said that perhaps there have been rather too many indifferent coaches in rugby over the years, but when a good one came along, such as Carwyn James, he could create for his team a magnificent brand of rugby, pleasurable for player and spectator alike. The good coaches allowed the talented players to operate within a flexible structure.

Today, many people term the exciting rugby of that era the Welsh way of playing. While that is not entirely accurate, we were encouraged to work out how to beat opponents. Over the years, great Welsh players such as D. Ken Jones and even Claude Davey back in the 1930s were strong running centres, with lovely side-steps and swerves. In addition to that, they had the ability to read a game, to beat people by working situations out. Before coaching came in, all that was simply left to chance. It was largely a question of luck whether players produced those skills on a particular day. The message coaches brought in the late 1960s was that in a team game everything needs to come right. Preparations prior to the game could assist that process. In those early coaching years, we practised basic moves to give us a better understanding of team work. It gave us the confidence to try moves. Prior to 1971, Wales had not won a Grand Slam since 1952, a gap of nineteen years. It is my belief that the opportunity to have squad sessions and a coach to take responsibility, guiding and encouraging us to play a certain type of game, allowed the talent among the players to flower in a very exciting manner which captivated the imagination.

I realise this may all sound a little naive but even that side of 1971 had no more than two set moves in its locker. Rugby was a pretty straightforward, simple game in those days, epitomised by Clive Rowlands' urgings when he was coach of the national team. 'Good ball, use it; bad ball, kick it' was his creed. He might add 'Go out and express yourselves' but that was about it. Clive utilised his experience of having played at the highest level and of having been an exceptional motivator. In those early days, he realised that we just needed winding up and then letting go. It was all light years away from the smoothly structured game of this day and age. Now, working on unit skills accounts for the majority of time spent in preparation. Sadly, however, I believe that in turning the modern-day players into very efficient performers, we have taken out of the game the one ingredient that is absolutely essential. That is, the process of thought – how to read a game, how to think for yourself and how to beat people.

It is too easy to blame referees and systems. It simply isn't appropriate to do that, in my view. The trouble was that once coaches became an accepted part of the vocabulary, each one would try to outdo the others. As a result, more and more theory came into the game, much of which was good but a great deal of which just confused the whole issue. I don't think we were well blessed right across the board with an abundance of good coaches. The good ones of the last twenty to thirty years, the really exceptional ones, you can easily count on the fingers of one hand.

The most essential requirement of a coach is to get the best out of his players and inspire them as a team. Some coaches seem to feel they can be measured by the amount of scientific material they can put into a player's head, and play a great game on paper. For me, Carwyn James was a great coach because he was a great man-manager. He was, in addition, a careful, brilliant student of the game, which he fully under-stood. He knew the way he wanted to play the game and how therefore to approach it. The great difficulty some coaches have is in not allowing players to do the things they do best. The chances are that if that 1971 Grand Slam team played today, they would be told to play in a certain manner which might not get the best out of them.

There have been and still are some fine coaches in world rugby. I always felt that the 1984 Australian Wallabies under Alan Jones played an up-dated version of the 1971 Lions style under Carwyn James. It was basically the way Wales played throughout the 1970s. The theory was if it was good ball move it and, above all, have the confidence to move it.

Jim Telfer has had plenty of good times with Scottish national teams. Jim's qualities have shown through as much when things have not looked promising for the Scots. For example, who would have forecast a Scottish Grand Slam in 1990, especially when England were busy carving up all-comers that season until they reached Murrayfield for the Grand Slam showdown? I detected Telfer's hand behind that triumph, as I have for several other worthy Scottish successes since, such as that famous 23–21 win over France in Paris in 1995, their first victory in the French capital since 1969 when Telfer himself was in the Scottish team. Jim Telfer's long contribution and service to both Scotland and the Lions give him fully merited entry into the lists of the all-time, outstanding coaches.

Scotland's Ian McGeechan achieved successes with the Lions in Australia (1989) and in South Africa (in 1997).

McGeechan was also, of course, Scotland's coach before he joined Northampton as Rugby Director and his outstanding coaching prowess was demonstrated when Scotland took that 1990 Grand Slam, under him and Jim Telfer. McGeechan also coached the 1993 Lions tourists to New Zealand and came within a whisker of winning that series, too. Those were notable achievements, confirming his reputation as a shrewd, pragmatic coach who worked meticulously to help his sides play to their utmost potential. And now he is back with Scotland as coach to plot new triumphs.

One man who helped McGeechan with the 1993 Lions was Dick Best, who had a great run with England and achieved some good results. He helped them become consistently successful until his sudden removal from office, which surprised many people in rugby, not just in England.

Pierre Villepreux has been something of a father-figure to the French in coaching terms and his teams have remained faithful to the tradition of French rugby. Bob Dwyer has had much international recognition, as has John Hart, although New Zealand's poor run of results in 1998 brought calls for the head of the All Black coach. I was glad he survived for I believe John has much to offer.

So, too, has Nick Mallett, the coach of South Africa. Nick took over when the world seemed to fall in on South African rugby – well, it seemed that way to the rugby-loving South Africans! After all, the Lions had just been to the Republic and won the Test series 2–1, and results like that do not go down very well at all in that land. Carel du Plessis paid the price as Springbok coach and Mallett was brought in. In no time at all, it seemed, South Africa were embarking upon their autumn 1998 tour of the UK and Ireland with a world record number of consecutive Test victories within their grasp. They beat Scotland, Wales and Ireland to match the seventeen once chalked up by the New Zealand All Blacks, but then they lost to England and the record was gone. What a fantastic turnaround Mallett had instigated, and in virtually no time at all.

Another southern hemisphere coach who, I am happy to say, is making an impact in Wales is Graham Henry, the New Zealander who coached Auckland through so many of their successful times in the early 1990s. He took over as Welsh national coach in the autumn of 1998. Henry is already instilling confidence in a Welsh team that had been dragged through the ashes of defeat. I hope Graham will encourage the type of game that is the very strength of Welsh rugby, a game of innovation and guile. It is still early days but the signs look promising, especially after that victory over South Africa.

Perhaps the acid test of a coach's skill is how his teams will be regarded with hindsight. What will be their legacy? What will they bequeath to those who follow?

Apart from the rule changes and the advent of coaches and coaching promoting an exciting style of play, the leading players of the day also made that era special. Take Barry John, for example. Let me try to explain Barry's unique qualities. He was so laid-back, so confident and had such a carefree attitude that it rubbed off on everyone around him. His famous statement made when we met for the first time and I asked him where he liked the ball to be delivered, summed him up perfectly: 'You just chuck it, I'll catch it.' And he did. That was Barry – tons of confidence and just as much skill.

When I first met Barry, he was exactly what I needed. I was a young kid dying to get on to the international scene but being heavily criticised for the weakness of my pass. Despite whatever other skills I might have possessed, it didn't seem to be coming together for me in terms of my pass. Once I met Barry, I quickly came to realise that it was a confidence problem. Barry gave me confidence by his attitude and I don't think I worried about passing ever again after that. I threw a few bad passes in my time to Barry and other outside-halves I played with, but Barry's confidence had rubbed off; I didn't let it concern me as I had before I'd seen his attitude and self-confidence.

We played together for Cardiff, Wales and the 1968 and 1971 British Lions. He broke his collar bone in the first Test of that '68 tour to South Africa which was a terrible shame because he could have shown so many people how he could play on that tour.

For me, Barry wasn't Welsh-like in his approach to the game. What I mean is he didn't follow the style and fit the physical stature of traditional Welsh fly-halves such as the great Cliff Morgan and David Watkins, of Newport, Wales and the 1966 British Lions. They were both small, very fast and nippy, tremendous side-steppers and jinkers who were into and through a gap in a twinkling. They formed a role model for Max Boyce's famous 'Fly-half Factory' which he immortalised in word and song. After them, Phil Bennett was another in that classic mould. Indeed, almost every Welsh village team seemed to have a small fly-half in that same style. It was taken for granted they could all side-step their way out of a paper bag.

Barry was different. Here was a taller, slim outside-half who tended to take the ball standing still, by and large. He was a subtler, more weaving type of player. He had exceptional skills and could read a game so thoroughly he could see things happening before they actually did. He was ahead of people in their thought process. He often wanted the ball almost static because he could ghost past people. He was much faster than he was given credit for. We would see this time and again in training on the athletics track. He was really quick, especially from a standing start. Yet there was an early reluctance to accommodate his type of fly-half skills. Of the modern generation, Neil Jenkins has suffered in the same way. It was not until Graham Henry arrived and showed his faith in Neil that we began to see his real skills demonstrated with complete confidence at international level.

Barry John had outstanding ability and was a highly gifted footballer in so many ways. He developed into a great goalkicker, too. Perhaps only those who saw him play on that 1971 Lions tour of New Zealand ever really understood just what a genius he was. Films from that time don't do him justice. All tour, he glided and ghosted majestically past defenders who were trying to knock his head off. He mesmerised defences; he was almost like a cobra. So many opponents on the field thought they had him, but he would almost vanish into space.

Barry was a sheer delight to play with and the best compliment I can pay him is that when he finished in 1972 after a mere six-year international career and twenty-five caps, I was thoroughly and deeply upset. I felt there was so much more to come from our partnership. I was only just beginning to mature as a player, being a couple of years younger than him, and some of the things that we were starting to do at Cardiff were really exciting, almost telepathic. I felt we could have gone on to become much better collectively and it was a colossal disappointment to me when he retired at twenty-seven. He was playing out of his skin at the time.

Of course he finished too early – he could have played almost to the end of the 1970s had he wished. But during the 1971 Lions tour, a monster called publicity was created that he found impossible to handle. In the end, that ogre destroyed his career. We all had to hold down jobs, and he also had to look after and provide for a young family plus dealing with all the pressure that came from rugby. Barry didn't enjoy the limelight, he wanted a simple life. He was never as happy as when he was having a pint or two with his mates and chatting about the game. But he felt people wouldn't leave him alone, he couldn't get away from all the attention. He didn't want the fuss everybody wanted to bestow upon him. I didn't feel resentment exactly at his decision to finish but I knew then it was wrong, and time has confirmed that view.

Barry is a proud, sometimes stubborn man and outwardly he would still profess that he got it right in finishing when he did. He'd never say he made a mistake. But on reflection, in the company of close friends, I know he is sorry he did what he did, especially as his friends went on to play for at least another six seasons. I am sure somewhere along the line he would have loved to have been out there with us, and he regretted not being able to.

I made one significant effort to get him to put aside his decision. In 1972, Cardiff were due to tour Rhodesia and I tried to persuade him to come on the tour with us. I felt it would get him away from the intensity of Wales and I thought I could change his mind while we were on that tour. But he said he didn't want to go and I concluded that his mind was made up.

The lucky thing for me and for Wales was that no sooner had Barry gone than up stepped an outside-half by the name of Phil

Bennett. He was a different type of player from Barry. The only thing that was the same with Barry and Phil was that they were both great players. Otherwise, everything was different – attitude, way of playing, character. Phil was a lot more introverted, a quieter person but a brilliant footballer, more in the Welsh mould like Cliff Morgan and Dai Watkins. He was a fantastic side-stepper but sometimes I don't think even Phil knew where his side-steps would take him, which made life desperately hard for defences to 'read' him.

I think it's true to say that the phrase 'Barry John and Gareth Edwards' became widely familiar both during and after that era. It's true we were club-mates at Cardiff, but the statistics show that I played more often for Wales with Phil Bennett as my outside-half than with Barry. Phil and I appeared in the same Welsh side twenty-nine times whereas Barry and I made twenty-three appearances together. But perhaps the fly-half who was the most important of all for me was Dai Watkins alongside whom I won my first two Welsh senior caps. His help and maturity ensured I got through to the next step.

My partnership with Phil Bennett took a lot more hard work than had been the case with Barry, because we weren't playing in the same club side. I had to start all over again with the partnership, but squad sessions were becoming regular by then and that helped us forge an understanding pretty quickly. Once Phil arrived, I had to start throwing the pass that bit harder to give him a fraction more space and time. Phil inspired those around him in the team by his ability to show brilliance out of nothing whereas Barry gave a more subtle message by what he did. Barry would joke a lot, it would always be, 'Don't worry, we'll sort it out.' Preparing for an international with Barry was never a problem whereas Phil would get much more nervous.

So we all felt the tension more than when Barry was around. Barry exuded complete confidence bordering on arrogance. His self-belief was legendary and in the end, there was nothing we felt we couldn't do alongside him. It may sound conceited although it's not meant to; we always felt in control of our game, even under the most severe pressure. There was always a feeling with Barry around that we would create something, or something would happen. Phil was more of an instinctive genius who, as I said, at times probably didn't even know where he was going. You just tried to get as close to him as you could to support.

When I look back at those times, it's the sheer thrill of playing with those guys that I remember most, seeing how they opened up tight defences and witnessing some of the tries they scored which defied their physique. I can still see Phil, burrowing like a little ferret up someone's trouser leg, as he disappeared between a forest of French legs to score a try in one match.

One of our secrets was that as a side, we were all very comfortable with one another. We became friends, closer than you would expect. So, although there were of course changes in the side, there was a backbone that ran right through the side in the 1970s. It included two more great backs, Gerald Davies and J.P.R. Williams.

Gerald is one of my favourite players of all time and someone with whom I shared a great affinity. I remember the first time I heard about him. Maureen's father said he had seen a brilliant boy from Loughborough College playing in a Welsh trial and I was intrigued to think who this might be. Of course, it turned out to be Gerald. When he left Loughborough, he played for Cardiff before going on to Cambridge

University, and eventually heading off to London and to join the great London Welsh side of that time.

Gerald is admired and remembered for his great attacking play and for scoring some fantastic tries. He was also a tenacious tackler. It didn't matter how big they were, very few people got past him. When you had someone like him in your side, you always felt he could create something even in an apparently hopeless situation. It was Clive Rowlands who changed him from a centre to a wing in 1969 and his renowned ability to side-step with such brilliance was a devastating part of his weaponry on the wing. What made him so dangerous to opponents was that when he side-stepped, he hardly changed pace. Indeed, it almost seemed as though he went faster.

I'll never forget one occasion I was with him, helping some schoolboys with tuition and tactics. We were half playing a sort of game and in the second half, Gerald was playing against me. I never minded tackling, I felt I was a good tackler so that when he got the ball and started running at me, I thought to myself, 'I know exactly what he is going to do.' I pushed him up against the touchline as tight as I could and prepared for the flashing side-step inside at which moment I was going to hit him with a hard tackle. Just when he appeared to have no other option but to come inside, he put on the after-burners and went past on the outside inches from the touchline, leaving me standing.

He was so quick and well balanced – you have to have great balance when you're moving at that pace. He was like a bird when it is flying – it hardly seems to make an adjustment yet it quickens its speed and darts in a totally different direction. If I am out on the moors shooting grouse, I often think of Gerald Davies. The grouse just flick their wings and they're gone, dipping away at speed. Gerald was just like that.

Then there was J.P.R. Williams, the last line of defence, the rock. So many images typified him: the clenched fists after hurling French wing Jean-François Gourdon into touch at Cardiff; the blood pouring down his cheek after being raked by John Ashworth, the New Zealander, at Bridgend; the head-band tying in his long hair during the Lions tour of 1974. Socks down, solid features set, he loved physical contact, almost wanted to test himself by being hurt. Above all else, he loved the challenge. Many full-backs confronted by a New Zealand pack of forwards would have had qualms about going up for the high kick ahead, knowing their fate when they collided with the strong men. JPR sought such challenges. If you went anywhere near a high ball, there would be this resounding cry of 'Mine'. A lion of a Lion, if you get my meaning.

His attitude, his sheer competitiveness was best demon-strated in one match against Ireland at Cardiff in March 1975. Ireland had arrived fancying their chances and in contention for the Championship but we played some great rugby that day and scored 32 points which was our biggest ever score against the Irish in Wales at that time. We managed five tries in all and produced some superb stuff. At 32–0 and the Championship won, the crowd were in fine voice, the songs rolling down the terraces of the old Arms Park. They wanted more of the magic and guess who thought he'd give them some. The ball came back to me off the top of a line-out and I thought I'd send it out to Phil Bennett in some style. I threw a reverse pass that seemed sure to capture the spirit of the moment, or so I thought. It was a brilliant idea except for the fact that the Irish No. 8, Willie Duggan, was lurking in the path of the ball, probably well offside. Willie caught it, unpenalised by the referee, and set off on a 25-yard run to our line for the only Irish score of the afternoon.

When we got back to the line to await the conversion, Phil was still laughing and I was grinning. After all, it was just about the last move of the match and we'd won a handsome victory. One man who wasn't laughing was JPR. He went absolutely mad at me. 'What the hell do you think you're doing?' he demanded. 'You've allowed them to cross *my* line,' he roared at me. I stood there like the errant pupil being bawled out by the headmaster. That summed up J.P.R. Williams. He never gave up, never stopped trying, never ever allowed himself to slip from the highest standards he set, which was why he was the player he was.

JPR would have played anywhere on the field, and often did on the training ground. Hooker, prop, back row, he didn't mind mixing it with the forwards and he would have been competitive enough to have made a decent fist of the job, too. One player not even he could have ousted was 'Merve the Swerve', one of the finest No. 8s Wales or the British Lions have ever been fortunate enough to select.

Mervyn Davies had class written all over him. Big, mobile, excellent with his hands, strong mentally and physically – there wasn't very much Mervyn couldn't do. He, just as much as JPR or Gerald or Barry or Phil, epitomised those Welsh teams of the 1970s, class players in key positions. Mervyn just got on with it, whatever the situation. He was a no-nonsense player who took the shoeing opponents would dish out (and there was plenty of it in those days) and continued to concentrate on his primary task: delivering good quality ball.

With Mervyn in the key ball delivery position of No. 8, it was no wonder we enjoyed so many good attacking options. As a youngster, he was a very good basketball player and those skills and hand-to-eye ball coordination served him nobly on the rugby field. He was a superb ball handler, so good at controlling the ball at the back of the line-out. He was also excellent at being in the right position just when you wanted him to be there. When illness struck him down and terminated his career early, Wales lost a superb player.

Another fine forward who was a great character of that era was Billy Mainwaring of Aberavon. Together, Billy and his mum could probably have conquered the world, so formidable were they! A few months ago, Mrs Mainwaring had her eightieth birthday and she and her son have been stalwarts of 'The Wizards' for as long as most can remember. Mrs Mainwaring has impeccable credentials for the title of 'rugby's best supporter'.

Parochialism was never better illustrated within Wales than at grounds like Llanelli's Stradey Park where the Sospans were regarded as the best side in Wales and probably the world, and the Talbot Athletic Ground, home of Aberavon, where smoke belched out of the chimneys of the local steel works. On a bad day when you played there, it would fill your lungs but the proud workforce who stood on the terraces and roared for the local team never seemed to mind.

After the initial shock of hearing Mrs Mainwaring's vocal support for the Wizards, you somehow felt in subsequent visits that if you weren't the recipient of her ridicule, you had missed out. She loved Billy, of course, but she also liked me, at least when I wasn't playing against Aberavon. I remember one famous occasion at the Talbot ground. Billy, who was a strong, powerful lock forward for the local club, had me in a fearsomely tight grip. At the very least, I thought dismemberment was probably imminent. Miraculously, I was saved not by some beefy Cardiff forward who came to my rescue, but the voice of dear Mrs Mainwaring in the stand. 'Put Gareth down, Billy,' came the unmistakable voice. 'He's playing against England next week.' And Billy, all 6 feet 4 inches of him, looked at her and looked at me, shook his head and meekly did what his mum said. My father who was there and heard it, simply cracked up!

I remember another match against Aberavon, a thoroughly abrasive Cup tie during which the Aberavon pack had given me a torrid time. Right at the end of the game, I suddenly found myself in the clear, having wriggled through almost the entire pack. Just one man remained to confront – Billy Mainwaring. I prepared to give him a hand-off but somehow my instincts told me he was going to let me have one. So in the split second before the palm of my hand was going to meet his chin, I closed it into a fist and cracked him straight on the mouth. It struck him so well my wrist almost went down his throat. Billy wasn't hurt, but he was certainly surprised. The referee, Jeff Kelleher, wagged a finger at me, although he was sympathetic because he knew what the Aberavon forwards had done to me that day. I had been pulled, punched, gouged, everything. Immediately he had finished talking to me, the referee blew the final whistle and the match was over. One thought worried me – what would Mrs Mainwaring say about me hitting her Billy? I saw her quite soon after and went up to her. 'I'm sorry for hitting Billy,' I said. And she replied, 'Never mind, Gareth bach, he must have deserved it.'

What bound all these great players and several others together and made us the success story we became was not, strangely enough, a manic desire to stuff England at every opportunity (although of course we wanted to beat them perhaps more than anyone else); nor was it necessarily a craving to give employment to the small army of factories which sprouted up in the Welsh valleys at that time to churn out sweaters with Triple Crown or Grand Slam logos on the breast. What brought us together, fuelled our collective desire and made us the team we were was a love for the game. We were young kids who just adored what we were doing and revelled in the thrill of it all. The players in those Welsh teams had the confidence, the attitude, the belief but more than that, we loved being out there playing the game.

I won't accept that we were an arrogant team. We weren't. For example, I can't think of one easy game we had against England in that era even though we beat them most times we played them. But the result on the scoreboard rarely tells the whole tale, and we had some extremely tough games with the English, both in Cardiff and at Twickenham. I strongly deny any charge of arrogance, because I believe our background prevented us from being that way. We were valley boys from close-knit communities and our friends would soon have put us in our place had we become big-headed. Most of us continued to live in those communities throughout our playing careers.

Something else convinces me we weren't arrogant. Had we been, I don't believe so many people would have such wonderful memories of that era. And I don't mean only Welsh people. Complete strangers all around the world have told me, and still do, how much they admired the way we played. They wouldn't do that had we had swollen heads. They wouldn't have bothered with us as soon as we'd retired from the game.

Being in a team with players you deeply respected, indeed admired for their skills was what made us gel. Like good actors, the players were all comfortable with one another. There was a lot of laughing, albeit mixed with a serious attitude when required, but it was more like a family going out to play together. That was how close we became. We all knew one another and cared for each other so that we never went out just thinking, 'We've got to win this to achieve another Grand Slam or Triple Crown or Championship title.' It went deeper than that for us.

I have mentioned elsewhere that it was a fear of losing that often kept me going. I didn't want to let anyone down, especially my team-mates. The crowd became a part of that so I felt that, if I failed, I'd be letting down my mates, my family, my club, my country. It increased the pressure but meant that the expectation of winning trophies was not all that counted, far from it.

We had our come-uppances from time to time; we didn't win every match. Losing a rugby match was, for me, like losing a fish – the ones that got away were the ones you remembered most. For example, we played abysmally in Dublin in 1970 and lost 14–0 to Ireland; in 1974 we lost 16–12 to England at Twickenham, which turned out to be England's only win over us in sixteen matches between 1964 and 1979. It was enough to cost us the Championship that season. In 1975, we played poorly to lose 12–10 in Scotland and in 1977, France beat us 16–9 in Paris to take the Grand Slam.

So we lost some matches yet there was a togetherness with the whole Welsh team. To win rugby matches you need many things, including good players and luck. We certainly had both of those very often, but to be consistent you need durability, and players for all seasons and circumstances. We had those players, and the glue which bound us all so close together made it especially difficult for opponents to break us or keep us all quiet. Opponents who succeeded in keeping some of us quiet in a match, perhaps by bottling up Barry John and myself or Phil Bennett and myself, would find the source of inspiration coming from someone else that day. Perhaps it would be JPR or Gerald, one of the centres, or even the back row. Someone else would emerge to make a decisive contribution.

We weren't a team that relied on one or two individuals – others could open up defences and then we'd be away. The All Blacks seem to have this quality whatever the era, and the last South African touring team to Britain had it. The French sides we saw in the 1999 Five Nations Championship definitely didn't have it!

There was something about that era which transcended parochialism. We didn't recognise it at the time but I think we gave something to the rugby-playing world. We are not the only sporting team to have done that, of course. Those great Liverpool soccer sides of the 1970s and 1980s did much the same in their sport. They espoused a style, established a method which caught the imagination and respect of others. Before them, the great Real Madrid soccer teams of the 1960s achieved something similar. The trouble was, as always seems to be the case in the world of coaching, those who followed may have shared the same nationality as their guru, but few offered similar capabilities as the master. In the wake of Carwyn James's success with the 1971 British Lions and then with the Llanelli teams of that era, everyone who had ever got off a train at Cardiff Central and had allegiance to Wales, tried to follow in Carwyn's footsteps. The world became infected with Welsh coaches, most of them after just a couple of weeks training on some sports course at a University such as Aberystwyth. Once that nonsense had ended, we had the New Zealand example. A near plague of New Zealanders descended on the British Isles in the wake of New Zealand's success in the inaugural World Cup of 1987, to show us how we should be coaching and bring fame and fortune to teams at every level. Well, that was the theory, at least. Some clubs did benefit from their influence, but an awful lot didn't, and found the exercise had been a costly failure.

Once Wales had made it plain that they would not be using Carwyn as their national coach, it was obvious we had squandered a colossal talent. Wales still tried to play in the same vein as Carwyn's '71 Lions but they found year on year that the sides they were meeting were better prepared and more effective defensively. They could cope with what Wales had to offer. We could handle that through the 1970s but after that, sadly, Wales didn't have anywhere to go; there was no one to plot a fresh, bright new future. It became that much more difficult to play an expansive game, a style which allowed players to use their natural talents. We managed it from time to time, but only intermittently.

Television has played an increasingly significant part from that era onwards. Not only were the Lions and the Welsh sides of the early 1970s successful, with players of world-class ability, but their skills were being seen by millions who might otherwise never have witnessed them. Rugby on TV made that Welsh team *the* team to beat. We were there for a decade and became household names.

Broadcasts of earlier Lions tours were, at best, patchy or simply non-existent. You had to rely on the daily newspaper, probably a day after the match had been played, to find out the details. Here was a major difference; rugby fans all around the world could see highlights of the games. Sports followers were witnessing the exploits of the Welsh rugby team and being influenced by it.

A year or so ago, when I was in Japan for the National Sevens tournament, I was introduced to someone who told me a remarkable story that underlines this point. This Japanese man said that, all those years earlier, he had played rugby and when he saw TV pictures of the Welsh team, decided to base his whole game on my play. He bought all the films and books he could lay his hands on and developed his game around my style of play. But he did a lot more than that. He travelled to Wales, and took a job working in a restaurant to enable him to go on a rugby course at Aberystwyth. For a time, too, he lived in Cardiff. He said he felt he had to go for the full fix to be part of it, that great era for rugby and Wales. So he spent months in Wales trying to get as much knowledge as he could about our rugby. To me, that story showed what an influence our rugby had, what that era meant to people.

Of course, to the youngster who may be reading these words and feeling a little baffled, I should explain that Sky Television was not around in those days, relaying live pictures of entire rugby internationals on the other side of the world and even, in the case of the 1997 Lions, every single game the Lions played on that tour; nor could you see Ashes Test matches fought out live on the TV screen in your living room, or an England cricket tour of the West Indies. So much has changed.

That television exposure, coupled with the change in the kicking laws a few years earlier, opened the game up to a whole new audience. The success of the Lions sides in the first half of the 1970s in New Zealand and South Africa gave the game a huge standing among young people. To an extent, it meant that we, the players on those tours, were among the first to become public property. The different reactions to our homecoming from the 1968 and 1971 Lions tours illustrate the point. In 1968, after being away for three and a half months in South Africa, I came home to find some people in my village bumping into me and saying, 'Gareth, haven't seen you for ages. Where have you been?' After flying into Heathrow, the Welsh boys on that tour found our way to Reading and caught the train to Wales. I got off at Neath and might even have got a bus up the valley to my village, I honestly can't remember now. Perhaps I walked. The point was, hardly anybody knew anything about it.

Three years later, when the '71 Lions' plane touched down at Heathrow after the tour, there was the biggest crowd of people at the airport since the Beatles came back from America. We literally fought our way through vast crowds, all cheering us and slapping us on the back. It was phenomenal and staggered us. There were buses and buses of supporters who had made the journey up from Wales and, in fact, they'd come from all over the British Isles and Ireland. I'd never seen or expected anything like it.

Wales was united by it; it made a huge impact. At Neath, when we eventually managed to force our way off the train, the whole station was jam-packed; I almost missed my mother and grandmother in the crush. A special convoy of cars took us eleven miles up the valley and the road was lined with cheering supporters the whole way. There was not a single village which hadn't turned out to welcome us.

Delme Thomas found exactly the same thing making his way home to Carmarthen. Others experienced something similar.

For the next four months, we went around the country like kings. The game had suddenly risen in public awareness. We were voted the Sports Team of the Year by the BBC's viewers and TV appearances were two-a-penny. We were received by the Lord Mayor in London and the Prime Minister at 10 Downing Street.

The point of all this is that rugby made a huge impact. The man who had plotted our success, Carwyn James, gained an enormous reputation among the public and rugby supporters. Suddenly, more and more kids were kicking rugby balls around. Then, just seventeen months later with many of the same personnel still involved, came that captivating Barbarians match against the 1973 New Zealanders at Cardiff. You only have to think of the impact that game still has on British rugby a quarter of a century later to realise that for those who played in it, the game was suddenly and dramatically changing in its public perception and popularity. It was inevitable that the players would become caught up in it all.

In faraway New Zealand, a small boy watched the highlights of that Barbarians game against his own countrymen, on television at home. Sean Fitzpatrick, destined to become one of New Zealand rugby's most distinguished and successful captains and hookers, said years later, 'That one game inspired me to take up rugby.'

Wherever I travel today, whether it is to Edinburgh or Auckland, Wellington or Dublin, Sydney or the Scottish Borders, Paris or London, the number of people who still talk about that match and the try I scored, astonishes me. People home in on that one game.

Twenty years after my retirement, I am constantly amazed at the way I am still asked about matches from that era. Far, far more people want to talk about those days than the modern era. I don't believe that is just because Wales have had some lean years in the intervening period. When I retired, I felt that if I got five years more recognition from my rugby-playing days, time in which I might be able to earn something of a living from TV work, after-dinner speaking, writing the occasional book and such like, I would be a happy man. After those five years, I felt I would be history, overtaken by the new kids on the block, which is the natural process, of course, the way of the world. Still to be doing all those things twenty years later leaves me astonished. All the spare time I was convinced I would have for hobbies such as fishing and shooting when my life became much quieter after those four or five years, has simply never materialised. Far from finding, as I expected, that I was gradually being left behind, I have found myself getting busier and busier.

I am certainly a little bewildered by it, but you won't hear me complaining. It has been wonderful to combine my hobbies with business. I travel worldwide to help promote the game and to speak at dinners and special events. I consider myself very fortunate when people come up and ask for my autograph or just to have a chat. To me, there is nothing nicer than a young person coming up and saying, 'Please may I have your autograph?' I have children of my own and know what it means.

It is possibly the greatest compliment anyone could pay regarding that era of rugby that such things are still happening today, twenty-five and more years afterwards. The players who were instrumental in bringing it about left a legacy which I hope will act as a challenge for future generations to match. It was a special era, in more ways than one. A glorious chapter of rugby was played out in those days. I am forever grateful for the fact that people still remember it, and acknowledge it for what it was. That means more to somebody who played a small part in it than any long-forgotten cups, trophies or titles.

CHAPTER SIX

How the Game Has Changed

The posts are the same, the pitch dimensions just about similar, but those elements apart, there isn't an awful lot about the game nowadays which reminds me of the sport I played.

There are those who cast only doom and gloom on most aspects of the sport today. Paying players was wrong, charging more for entrance was wrong, allowing money from business entrepreneurs to flow into the game was wrong, letting professionalism darken the whole game was wrong, and so on and so on. I don't agree with any of that. There are plenty of things about present-day rugby that are considerable improvements on the game I knew.

Take fitness levels. If we thought we were in pretty good shape around the 1970s, able to play the game at a reasonably fast pace and maintain it for the full eighty minutes, the example of the modern-day player makes us think again. These guys are in fantastic condition. They handle the ferocious intensity of the tackles, make the big hits themselves and run all afternoon. Rugby today is much more physical than ever before and I take my hat off to the players who are producing their skills in such an environment. It cannot be easy.

I would be lying if I said absolutely everything about the game is just the way I would like it to be. Certain things cause me concern and I question the motives behind some of the changes that have been made to the fundamental structures of the game.

The question of whether the game should have gone professional is a completely separate debate, which is the subject of a later chapter. Briefly, I feel that there was little choice if rugby union was to retain its reputation for honesty and integrity. Huge sums of money were coming into the sport, and more and more demands were being placed upon the players. Of course, that was by no means a new equation. Back in 1977 when I was still playing, much pressure had been put on me to make a fourth tour with the British Lions, to New Zealand. But I had been on three Lions tours already by that stage and was mindful of the need to start thinking about my future and making plans accordingly. The pressure to persuade me was intense, but I resisted it. Several other players were in a similar position. Some had been unable to accept a single invitation to make a Lions tour because of business and/or family commitments. Even then, so much time was being demanded of the leading players that many began to feel uncomfortable about being away from their work so often. Twenty years earlier, the prestige and kudos of having an employee chosen for a Lions tour was such that a company would actually encourage rugby men to go on the tour. By the time I was coming to the end of my career, that was not the case.

I retired in 1978 but between then and 1995 when professional rugby was born, there was a gross contradiction.
Throughout that time, players were being told they had to be
professional about the way they played and prepared for
matches, without receiving a penny. The unions and clubs were
raking in millions of pounds from sponsors, and none of that
money was going to the players; not officially, anyway. It had
become an untenable situation for a sport that had always
prided itself on its openness and honesty.

What I regret about professionalism is the way it was brought
in, not its arrival *per se*. That was inevitable. I bemoan the years
of in-fighting between unions and clubs which followed and the
resultant damage to the game's fine reputation which had been
built up over more than a hundred years.

So professionalism arrived, which was not necessarily a bad
thing, but what followed was a more disturbing trend – the
constant tampering with the laws of the game. I am inclined to
ask of certain people in authority today around the world, do
they really understand the game, are they aware of its history,
its traditions, its styles and what made it great? Or have they
come from a background outside the game and are now
involved because they bring a commercial knowledge to rugby?
If the latter is true, it ought to concern us all that some may
have played a role in altering specific laws of the game which
have helped to make a serious difference to the sport I knew as
a player.

In fairness, I must cite one aspect of the game which has
changed for the better. In my time, you almost had to kill an
opponent for your side to be awarded a penalty try. Today, far
more penalty tries are awarded and although I have certain
misgivings about the entire process – because who on earth can

really say a try probably would have been scored (a player can always drop a ball over the line and many do, frequently) – at least the ultimate sanction is there if a side deliberately transgresses to prevent an opponent scoring. That form of cheating is wilful and deserves to be strictly punished. Referees use that power far more in the modern game than years ago and so they should to stop the professional foul.

My main concern with the modern game relates to two key phases of play: the scrummage and the line-out. Let's look at the scrummage first. When professionalism first arrived, and the southern hemisphere gave the lead by producing an altogether faster, slicker and more open game, a view seemed to grow up that the scrum was no longer important. Some saw it solely as a means of getting the game going again. I am pleased to see that in the last eighteen months, certainly in the northern hemisphere, there has clearly been something of a re-think of that view. In Wales, the value of a strong scrummaging pack was vividly emphasised when Argentina played at Llanelli in late 1998 and gave the Welsh pack a torrid night through their excellent scrummaging technique and great power. Wales were without Dai Young and Peter Rogers, two experienced and strong props who could have helped negate some of the power of that Argentine scrummage. But what Argentina did emphasised the continuing importance of a good scrum. Others, too, have acknowledged this point in recent times.

For example, Ian McGeechan re-built his Northampton forward pack in 1998–9 around the immensely strong South African international Garry Pagel, and a fine job the 1995 World Cup winner did for them. Pagel's scrummaging strength and technique were a test for all opponents and enabled his club to erect a solid base up front on which other component parts of the team could develop and play.

Without that solidity up front, not much else can work. The back row cannot detach immediately the ball has gone and attack the opposition half-backs, because their weight and strength are needed to prevent the front five from being shunted too far back. And if their scrum has been under pressure they will inevitably be on the back foot, and more physically tired too due to the effort involved at the set scrums.

Then, the scrum-half is under intense pressure all the time and his options for attacks, such as the blindside raid, are severely reduced. Trying to clear the ball from a pack that is under pressure and hurting backwards is the stuff of nightmares as far as scrum-halves are concerned.

I can recall to this day some of the powerful scrummaging teams and individuals that I played against in my career. In one Barbarians match against the touring South Africans in season 1969–70, two prop forwards, Moff Myburgh and Hannes Marais formed a massively strong front row unit against us. The pressure put on our scrum was so intense that our hooker, the Scottish international Frank Laidlaw, could not get his foot free to hook for the ball, so low were Myburgh and Marais taking the scrum.

'Gareth,' he called to me, before one scrum. 'I can't use my leg because we're being taken down so low. I'll hook the ball with my head,' which was what he proceeded to do. It was the most extraordinary sight and also an act of fair courage because a stray boot could have done a lot of damage to Frank in that position.

The law changes which decreed that scrummages had to stay higher, roughly at hip level, were brought in to prevent serious injury to anyone caught in a collapsing scrum. It is a dangerous place and players trapped in a collapsed scrum have sometimes been seriously injured. I applaud every effort to make the scrum safer. To hear of young men paralysed for life is sickening for anyone who ever played or watched the game. I was firmly behind the administrators who listened to experts and drew up law changes intended to make it safer.

However, the trouble with some changes that have been made is that they have altered the unique appeal of the scrum. Rugby union, because it had some quirky elements like the scrum and the line-out, was a game that suited sportsmen of all shapes and sizes. The short, fat individual could be an ideal build for a front row forward; the tall, lanky figure would be an ideal line-out player. Short and tall, fat and slim, fast and, shall we say slower – the fact that all these could play the game made it unique. But today, there are fewer ferocious scrummagers in the game. That has meant there's been a need for more mobile prop forwards which has encouraged a move away from the small, lumbering, heavy man to the somewhat more adroit, speedy and loose player. By and large, scrummages are not as fiercely contested as they once were and I, for one, regret that.

What has not changed is the almost total lack of knowledge of what goes on in the murky depths of a scrummage, a world where no outsiders are welcome and where strange, perhaps almost tribal laws exist. Who, for example, can point a precise finger of blame at one individual if a scrummage goes down? In my experience, hardly any referee has a clue who the culprit is. The world of the front rows is inhabited by some of the wiliest, most cunning and amusing men you will ever encounter on a rugby field. Take that famous old Welsh front row, popularly known as the VietGwent, because they all played for Pontypool, the Gwent club. Loose-head prop Charlie Faulkner, Bobby

Windsor who was the hooker and Graham Price, the tight-head prop, were all very different characters.

Pricey was the strong, silent one who hardly ever said anything but just got on with his job. When he did open his mouth, what Pricey said was always worth listening to. Bobby was king of the one-liners, a man able to make you crack up at any time of the day or night. Charlie had a logic that was all his own and lovely way about him. When they said anything, you knew there was more to it than just a simple statement.

I remember we once went up to Scotland to play at Murrayfield against a team that contained those two tremendous Scots and British Lions in the front row, Ian 'Mighty Mouse' McLauchlan and Sandy Carmichael. Sandy had both cheekbones shattered by punches from forwards of New Zealand's Canterbury provincial side a few days before the first Test of the 1971 British Lions tour. There is a famous picture of him with deep black swellings under both eyes, the after-effects of the fractured cheekbones. Questions were asked about the Welsh scrummage in the week leading up to that Five Nations match. Had we the power to hold them? At a team meeting at eleven o'clock on the morning of the match at our Edinburgh hotel, we discussed it. When we came out of the room and I asked him what he thought would happen, I remember Charlie Faulkner, in his inimitable drawl, coming out with this immortal answer.

'Well, Gar,' he said, 'we may go up, we may go down, but we're not going bloody back!'

For me, that typified prop forwards. They were always a breed who played the same way whether you were involved in an intense, high-pressured international match or just a training session. Before one international in Cardiff, we arranged a training session, with the boys from the South Wales Police XV providing 'live' opposition. I took the ball into one ruck and was probably a bit over the wrong side. The next thing I knew boots were raining in on me. I couldn't believe it – the international was only two days away. But it was black or white for those boys. When we protested, they said, 'If you're on the wrong side, you're going to have it.' And that was it. It didn't matter to them whether we were playing South Africa or New Zealand the next day. That typified their character.

The humour of the front row boys was legendary. Still is to this day, I'm certain of that. Who could forget the exploits of the English prop forward Colin Smart after a France–England game in Paris? A company involved in men's toiletries offered the players a free miniature bottle of aftershave each as a gift. The bottles were on the dinner table at the after-match banquet. Another England player, lock forward Maurice Colclough so it is thought, came up with a devious plan. He slipped into the dining room well before anyone else, found his seat and took the bottle to the washroom where he emptied the contents down the sink. He washed it out thoroughly, re-filled it with water, and replaced it beside his allotted place on the table.

The players subsequently filed in for dinner and found where they were sitting. Colclough, picking up his bottle of aftershave, challenged Colin Smart to down it in one. Most players apparently watched aghast, as Colclough put the 'aftershave' to his lips and drank the bottle. Smart was next and had no choice – he had to follow suit. Alas, his was the genuine thing. It wasn't long before he began to feel ill and was subsequently rushed to hospital to have his stomach pumped out. Prop forwards . . .

Another was the Irishman Phil O'Callaghan, who once came

to Cardiff to play in an invitation match against a Welsh XV to mark the opening of a new stand at Cardiff Arms Park. Everything and everyone were in carnival mood, the sun shone, the grass was a vivid green and there was an air of celebration and happiness. And then the first scrum went down. With all front row forwards, it is a simple matter of confrontation. Thus, at the first scrum, O'Callaghan drove his head right under the throat of our hooker Jeff Young. There was a loud blast on the whistle and referee Meirion Joseph penalised O'Callaghan for boring in, a technical offence committed by props targeting the opposing hooker. Another few minutes went by and another scrum broke up after a loud blast on the whistle. Joseph wagged his finger at O'Callaghan for the same offence. At this stage, most mortals would get the message and perhaps desist from further such activities. But not prop forwards. Ten minutes later, O'Callaghan drove his head right across the scrum at Young's head and the whistle went once more.

'You're boring again, O'Callaghan – I've warned you, now pack it up,' said the referee sternly. To which O'Callaghan replied in his lovely Irish voice, 'Ah, to be sure ref, you're not so exciting yourself.'

I think it was Phil O'Callaghan who was on the bench when an Irish team played Scotland. When a prop was injured, they called for O'Callaghan. 'Yer man', as they say, ran out on to the field but was suddenly seen to stop and stoop down as though picking something up. His packet of fags and matches had fallen out of his pocket!

When I played I was, of course, closer to a collapsing scrum than most players, yet I never had the slightest idea who was responsible. Referees are just the same. All they do is give one penalty to one side and the next penalty to the other side. In other words, they are fair but they can't call it being correct because they find it impossible to apportion proper blame. So much kidology goes on among front row forwards. These guys are cunning and wily; few fools exist in their secretive world. They regularly deceive everyone – referee, fellow players, spectators. I defy anyone outside a scrum to say they know just what is going on in there. Indeed, some old front row men have told me even they cannot tell just by watching a match.

In the old days, it was the tight-head prop's job to scrum his opposite number, the loose-head, into the ground and keep him as low as possible. He would also try to attack the opposing hooker by scrummaging across directly into him and squeezing aside that hooker's loose-head prop. But sometimes these tactics have not applied. What the French did in the 1980s and 1990s was damaging to the whole ethos of scrummaging technique. They decided that it didn't matter whether or not they had a technician playing at hooker and so they would choose three enormously powerful men in the front row and call one of them a hooker. Quite often he wasn't a hooker at all, but a prop. Then, in the early 1990s, they began to feel that it was worth sacrificing a hooker for a player with speed. So a player like Jean-François Tordo moved from open-side flank forward to hooker in international rugby, a startling transformation which challenged the very tradition of that part of the scrummage.

This worried me. I felt we were mucking around with the fundamentals of the game, something we do at our peril. I do not reject change out of hand but I am reluctant to see things that threaten the traditions of a sport.

One of the finest technicians I ever knew as a hooker during my playing days was a man who never won a single cap for Wales at senior international level. Yet on the club circuit in those days, the name of Moralais Williams of Neath was respected in every valley, every major rugby-playing town in the country. Williams would take strikes against the head from even the best hookers in the business. Many didn't like it and reacted violently because in the code of the front row men, their pride had been hurt. But that was the way it was, and for me it encapsulated rugby's wonderfully different qualities and aspects. Some world-class players blocked Williams's path to a Welsh cap, but he was nevertheless a fine hooker.

In times gone by, props had to do their grafting in the scrummage to secure their side's ball and perhaps take a strike against the head from their opponents. But today, it isn't anything like as strong a test for prop forwards, certainly not in southern hemisphere rugby. There, they just want to get the ball in and out. There isn't time for the technically proficient tight-head prop to do his stuff and wreck the opposition ball. Tackling and ball carrying seem to have become more important for a prop than scrummaging. I regret that. I still feel that props should have to work for their scrummage ball. Of course, not everything about the scrummage could be termed aesthetically pleasing. The irritating trick of twisting a scrum round so that it eventually has to be re-formed and the whole process endured a second or even third time, is a complete waste of effort.

One problem which does undermine the modern game can be directly attributed to the de-powering of the scrum. By common consent, there is a complete lack of space in the game we see today, chiefly in the midfield for outside-halves and centres. That whole area of the field is largely cluttered up from first to last, and one reason for it is that the forwards are not expending the same energy levels in the set scrums. That leaves them with the gas to get out wide and block up midfield much more than used to be the case.

If ever a country emphasised the continuing value of a good hard scrummage it was England in their match against South Africa at Twickenham in December 1998. The excellent English pack squeezed the scrums and caused the South Africans problems, often giving them bad ball to work from. It showed that proper, traditional scrummaging should still be a really important part of the game.

Another area in which modern rugby has moved away from its roots, to a worrying extent in my view, is the line-out. To see most teams not even bothering to contest line-out ball these days represents a complete desertion of the traditional battle for the ball in this phase of the game. With lifting now legal, there is virtually no way that the team throwing in the ball can lose possession. The only way is by a rank bad throw into the arms of an opponent or by a crooked throw, necessitating a scrummage. Otherwise, the advantage is one hundred per cent with the team throwing in and for me, that is a shame.

Perhaps lifting is a skill, but it has to be much less of a one than jumping; pure jumping was the acid test for line-out men. The game produced some classical exponents of the art; from Wales two in particular come to mind, Delme Thomas and Robert Norster. Delme Thomas was an outstanding jumper – strong, aggressive and powerful yet able to get genuinely high by his own efforts and secure quality ball. He could deliver it off the top of the line-out, too; that is, the ball would be flicked down to me, two-handed, while he was at the highest point of his jump, or even delivered accurately one-handed, with a flick. I always regarded that as the best possible ball with which to launch attacks. No opponent got within two yards of Barry

John when that kind of quality ball was deflected down to me and I fired it out.

Delme was a fine practitioner of his art and, believe me, it was an art. To rise high above everyone else with an opponent trying to stand on your feet to prevent you getting off the ground, or pulling your shirt or shorts to try and restrict the height you could reach, or even grabbing part of your body to make it more difficult and much more painful to rise high in the line-out, took some doing. I always had the greatest respect for such a fine line-out player as Delme.

Robert Norster, from my club, Cardiff, followed in the same classical steps as Delme, and Wales were fortunate to have two such talented players in that phase of the game.

What the line-out offered more than anything else was a role in the game for the lanky 6 foot 5 inch player who would have found it difficult to fit in anywhere else in the side. In some cases, the line-out men were even bigger; Peter Stagg, the former Scottish international lock, was 6 feet 10 inches tall. But he didn't win the ball automatically despite such an advantage because line-outs were contests. Often, a line-out would be decided by how well a supporting player, probably a prop forward, did his job in blocking off those opponents trying to get at his team's chief line-out man to disrupt his leap and intended catch.

The throw-in, of course, was and is so important, as we found to our cost in 1968 with the British Lions in South Africa when Frik du Preez, at just 6 feet 2 inches, through his fantastic leap and precise timing, regularly out-manoeuvred Peter Stagg.

The line-out was an area which demanded team skills. Whatever your size, you had a role to play in helping your colleague, and it was the side that contributed most in that sense that usually ended up with the ball. I find it faintly absurd today to see two players lifting a guy into the heavens, keeping him suspended there as though he were on the end of a huge rubber rope and the opposition just standing around waiting for him to come down, before becoming involved. That cannot be what the line-out was ever intended to be.

As with the scrummage, there are elements of this which have a knock-on effect in other parts of the field. Is it any wonder that suddenly back row forwards are appearing in the second row, like England's former No. 8 Tim Rodber? If you have more mobile players moving into the second row, they are there for another reason – to get around the field far more, and make tackles out wide. In other words, you end up with more forwards rumbling around the field and cluttering up any space which might have existed. Some teams have moved flankers up to lock to get the best of both worlds. The consequences of these very significant changes for the game as a whole are profound.

I don't challenge the assertion that the side kicking the ball out of play should lose possession, but with the laws as they are now, things have gone too far the other way. It's one thing to give an advantage to the attacking side but is it necessary to guarantee them possession? And what is the point of having a line-out anyway if you are virtually certain to win the ball? And if we abolish line-outs because they are perceived as a waste of time, how long will it be before we say scrums should not be contested and they are eventually dropped?

Already, many people are beginning to ask what is the need for really big men in their team. By big, I don't mean in terms of weight, but the really tall men, like Peter Stagg, Robert Norster, Wade Dooley and Martin Bayfield. If you can lift a colleague legally, you don't need huge men. A player of ordinary size, say 6 feet 2 or 3 inches, is perfectly tall enough if he is going to be lifted at the line-out.

So I am left to wonder whether the game will continue to be described as one for all shapes and sizes. If the props need to be fast runners and good ball handlers rather than solid scrummagers, and the line-out men just need to fizz about the field rather than be commandingly tall to win the ball, you are starting to threaten two distinct species of player who have always found a place in the game. This worries me, because it is surely a very short step to reducing the side to thirteen players. I suppose some may say that does not follow because fifteen-a-side is one of the fundamentals of the union game. So were a strong scrummage and a competitive line-out. They have largely been destroyed – might not the fifteen men change, too, if someone decrees that to be what is euphemistically termed 'in the interests of the game'?

In whose interests? Not those of the traditional rugby union man, the player or supporter who has been keenly involved for many years. It might suit the commercial eye of some entrepreneurial figure to reduce a team's numbers to thirteen. But if you start to erode the basic principles of the game and nothing is regarded as sacrosanct, there is no way of knowing where you will end up. If rugby continues down this path, it is not hard to see a scenario where every forward, indeed almost all players, will be around 6 feet 2 to 3 inches, weigh between 13 and 15 stone and there are only thirteen players in a team. They would be lined up across the field, all hammering into one another, with scrums a formality.

If any of this sounds familiar, so it should. I am describing the game of rugby league, a sport where really tall men do not have a role and the scrummage is seen primarily as just a means of re-starting the game. But even with only thirteen men in a rugby league team, sides still find it hard to break down defences.

I do not wish to knock rugby league, certainly the modern version. It is a game I might have enjoyed playing myself. I had the chance – Wigan and St Helens both made me very good offers early in my career and I considered them carefully. I never went north to discuss it, they came to see me at my home. I remember a big car drew up outside the house and these gentlemen got out and came inside. I was nervous about it all. The biggest drawback for us all was the stigma of 'going north', as they called it. There had been stories of players seduced by suitcases stuffed full of fivers or ten pound notes, but then finding they had been shunned, ostracised by their whole community back in Wales. Doubtless these stories had been embellished down the years to make people think twice. I certainly think they had an effect on me in my early days. So when the Wigan people called and asked to come down and see me, I said, 'OK, but I'm not really interested.' I remember they were very courteous, understanding and gentlemanly. They said to me, 'Name your price. What would you want to come?' I remember thinking, 'What the hell am I going to say now?'

The record at that time was the £17,000 David Watkins had been offered to go to Salford in 1967, a deal he had accepted. This was about two years later, so I told them they would have to be talking at least £20,000 for me even to consider it. Frankly, I didn't want them to make me an offer, but they said, 'All right.' I wasn't sure I wanted to play league because I was happy with my friends in Wales and happy playing for Wales which was something I had always wanted to do. I was also worried about 'oop north'. I didn't have a clue where Wigan was and I imagined just belching chimneys and factories with no nice places to live. It seemed so far away pre-motorways in 1969, and it was.

In those days, the league clubs really only wanted union boys when they were very young, and could be signed on long-term contracts. That changed over the years so that some Welsh players went when they'd had years of playing for Wales. Another change was in rugby league itself – the game is far better today than it was when I was twenty-one. I would have enjoyed the modern league game and it might have suited my style of play.

In the end, I think they were put off pursuing me any more when I said to them, 'I'm not really interested; the only reason I would come is for the money.' Had I been twenty-six or twenty-seven it's possible I would have gone. Having a family changes your outlook on all sorts of things. But it was too early when I did have the chance. I had too much still to hope for in rugby union. And I have to say, I've never looked back on those times and regretted my decision.

Today, I still love rugby union and don't want to see it changed into rugby league. However, if trends continue, it is heading that way. By exploring these points, I want to demonstrate the dangers of tampering so fundamentally with essential elements of our game, elements which have played a notable part for over a century.

Let me give you an example. In my time as a player, one of the best law changes made was the restriction on kicking to touch, a change which was responsible for opening the game up. Making lifting legal in the line-out has resulted in many more penalties being kicked into touch. Where we would tap the ball and run it, now teams kick it into touch as deep in the opposition 22 as possible, and try to launch a mauling drive for the try-line. It has become a tedious tactic.

Sides only do it because they know they are all but guaranteed the ball at the line-out. If the line-outs were contested and lifting outlawed, would everyone be so keen to kick away the ball, unsure of whether they would regain it at the subsequent line-out? The chances are they would tap the ball and start running, which would open the game up a great deal more. We would probably see more tries scored by the backs than by mauling forwards crashing over the line after the line-out.

The concerns I have are mainly about where these changes are taking us. Are we fast losing the game as we have known it? Are we allowing the southern hemisphere nations who have their own reasons for wishing to alter the fundamentals of the sport, to dictate to us and force us down their chosen road?

In Australia, people are used to flowing rugby with massive hits by the tackler on the ball carrier, and scrums that mean precious little. It is called rugby league. But it seems to me that because of their worry over league's greater support and in a bid to attract more followers themselves, rugby union in Australia has sought to ape the league game. That doesn't mean they should be allowed to dictate fundamental law changes to the rest of the world.

In late 1998, I found myself in Singapore at a rugby World Cup function. I had gone there to help the Welsh Tourist Board promote the tournament and I sat fascinated at a seminar concerning refereeing in the game when someone asked, 'What interpretation will we have for the 1999 World Cup?' I was so astonished I almost put my own hand up. What I would have said was simple: 'I was under the impression that there is only one set of laws in the game, not sets of interpretations.'

The development of competitions such as the Super 12 tournament in the southern hemisphere has created an even greater difference in interpretations. But is everyone happy to play the game that way? Or do others think, as I do, that many of the traditional aspects of the sport have been eroded, overlooked or bypassed in a crusade to produce only hectic, constant running rugby?

I do not subscribe to the view of some that Super 12 rugby is just candyfloss nonsense, but there's no doubt it has evolved into a type of basketball rugby with so much scoring going on. It is like one-day cricket, a bit soft here and there. While I admire the skills and tenacity of some of the play, the ball hardly stays with any player. I don't think the game was meant to be played like that. It wasn't intended to be a game where a team could maintain possession for fifteen minutes, or for as long as it took them either to score or make a mistake and lose possession. For that is how the laws are now set up, to hand all the advantages to the side in possession. Carry on like that and we might end up like the Dallas Cowboys with offensive and defensive units.

For me, the game is one of nip and tuck, changing defence into attack, winning the ball under pressure and using your skills to do something unexpected. A game should ebb and flow. For sure, Super 12 rugby is related to the proper game, but it is a very different version and no one can pretend otherwise.

I detect the hand of television behind all this. Without TV money, professional rugby union would be unable to survive in its present form. TV money plays a huge part in the success and development of the game. It also tends to dictate a certain approach. Already, we have seen throughout the world a huge increase in the number of internationals being played, and that is purely down to the demands of TV. It bothers me, too, that the game's best players are being made to play week in, week out. This glut of international matches has become so intense that the spectators are beginning to think, 'Oh no, not another international next week.' The South African tour of the United Kingdom and Ireland in late 1998 was a case in point. To play four internationals on four consecutive Saturdays was an astonishing schedule. It made physical demands upon players with which they clearly could not cope. It cannot have been surprising that England beat them on the last of those four Saturdays, after Wales and Ireland in particular had come close to doing so.

The South Africans' trip came at the end of a gruelling year which had started for their leading players with Super 12 warm-up matches at the beginning of February. That meant their top players had ten months of solid, competitive rugby at the highest level. No one can handle that kind of intensive programme and keep winning.

International rugby should always produce a sense of occasion rather than be just another game. But once lucrative TV contracts are signed, television requirements must be met. This is the reality of commercial life.

Most of the changes in the game I have outlined here have undoubtedly been encouraged by the influence of the TV people and those in authority within the game who have come on board in recent times, some since professionalism. Many have never been involved in the sport in their lives and sometimes you wonder what sort of people they are to make calamitous decisions such as England's four-Test tour of the southern hemisphere in the summer of 1998. Anyone who knew the first thing about rugby would have known that programme was a disaster in the making, mission impossible. But you could almost hear the reasoning of people in authority who didn't understand the sport and what it entailed. 'Well, they're going to be in New Zealand so they surely could stop off in Australia on the way and play them first. And if we're going to play Australia *and* New Zealand on the trip, well doesn't it make sense to complete the southern hemisphere experience and play South Africa on the way home?'

As a player who toured a fair amount and came to understand the physical demands such travel places upon the human body, not to mention the battering it takes when you get off the plane and start playing rugby in that part of the world, I have no time for officials who arrange such schedules. They don't understand the game or if they do, they have no feel for the players involved.

Perhaps the worst thing about all this is that those officials who should know better are being influenced by outside pressure. That is sad.

My concern is for the players. There are only so many matches in them.

The overall influence a figure like Rupert Murdoch can wield is frightening. Almost overnight, he virtually changed the game that had been run in a similar way for about a hundred years. The moguls were obviously fighting over it and although there had been countless rumours of breakaways from the amateur game, it was Murdoch's initial breakthrough with the Tri-Nations competition during the 1995 World Cup in South Africa that radically altered the sport. The Super 12 game has clearly been developed for TV audiences in the southern hemisphere. The vast injection of finance led to a concentration on international rugby and very quickly established a competition that would appeal to TV audiences. The trouble is that while in theory it remains the International Rugby Board's responsibility to govern the game worldwide, the reality is that when the Murdochs of this world say 'Jump', these people say meekly 'How far?'

As for the playing side, rugby needs to learn a particular lesson before the 1999 World Cup and I believe it should follow the example of the soccer authorities prior to their World Cup in France in 1998. They made it clear that there would be a systematic crackdown on certain key aspects of the game, such as tackling from behind, and all referees were instructed to be red hot on it. Rugby's rulers must do the same and the area I would like to see targeted is persistent offside. I do not like the effect of white cards, because having players going off for ten minutes takes something away from the whole game. On the other hand, you cannot allow illegal interference to prevent release of possession. Persistent offenders should be sent off because quick ball that offers opportunities to three-quarters is a fundamental part of the game.

Everybody sails as close to the wind as they can, that is to be expected. But a good referee should be able to sort out the persistent offender and enforce the law. Players are much fitter nowadays and therefore teams can absorb pressure for far longer periods. They are much better organised, too. So when fast ball is produced, it ought to be allowed to get down the line.

Defences have improved ten-fold and as time goes on it will become even more difficult to score. At the moment, not every team have good tacklers but everybody is moving towards being so. Then what will we have? Gridlock on the rugby field? It seems to me that we have caused this problem by bringing in rugby league people to assist in coaching union teams. While I do not deny that Phil Larder has done a very effective job in stiffening England's defences, so much so that neither Australia nor South Africa could score a single try against them in autumn 1998, I believe it is right to point out that the whole ethos of rugby league, the whole strut on which their game has been based, is defence. Are we saying that we in rugby union want to go down that same road?

These are the concerns I have as the game continues to change. At the moment, rugby union appears to have become a cross between rugby league and American football – stop, start, bang it down, chuck it here, chuck it there. At times, it's hard to recognise the old game we knew.

CHAPTER SEVEN

The Great Players and Teams

I t's a never-ending debate. Would the stars of yesteryear have handled the pressures of the modern game? Who was the greatest – J.P.R. Williams or Serge Blanco, Matthews or Best or Giggs? And what of the golfers – could Bobby Jones have negotiated the demands of the modern tour? Who was better – Jones or Jack Nicklaus or Tiger Woods? In rugby union, this subject has taken on a new lease of life since the sport turned professional. three years ago. I am constantly being asked which of the great old players do I think would have done well in the modern game, which ones would have excelled and perhaps been even bigger stars.

I can tell you, the way my knees feel some mornings, this 'old 'un' wouldn't have been able to live with the modern breed! But seriously, I always give people who ask me this the same reply. Great players would be great in any era. They would have the capacity to adapt to whatever styles were in vogue within the game. We are talking of players with a high level of skills, whether it be handling, running, kicking, passing or scrummaging. I am convinced that those at the peak of their sport in any era would be so today. Take J.P.R. Williams. JPR was a tough, extremely physical full-back who loved the challenge of a strong tackle, whether he was making it or taking it. Such a player would suit perfectly the modern professional game with its requirement for physical strength and explosive power.

I saw JPR hammer opponents in the tackle, sometimes leaving them a wreck on the ground. It was done perfectly legally but such was the ferocity of some of his defence, that players often wished they'd never gone anywhere near him.

When I think of some of the great New Zealand forwards who graced the game in my time, I cannot believe that they would not have been even more formidable in the modern game. I am thinking especially of Ian Kirkpatrick, that hard, fast, mobile, ball-handling back row forward, who is destined forever to be remembered as the man who played in that memorable Barbarians–New Zealand end-of-tour match at Cardiff Arms Park at the beginning of the 1970s. All over the world, rugby fans want to talk to the players who were there that day, about that match. For poor old Kirkie, it's like a nightmare that will never end. 'What a fantastic game it was,' I remember someone saying to him when I was in his company once.

'It might have been fantastic for you to watch, but I can assure you it wasn't fantastic to play in and lose,' he replied.

Then there was Colin Meads, a mighty man with a fearsome reputation. Meads was one of the strongest players I ever knew, as hard as nails. Don't tell me there wouldn't have been a place in the modern game for a player like him. Indeed, Meads was 'only' (daft word that, really, when you use it in connection with this immense man) 6 feet 3 inches tall, which was thought to be a bit on the small side by some of those who followed. In comparison with some of the 6 foot 8 inch to 6 foot 10 inch brigade, I suppose it was. But Meads was a colossus of a man in every other sense, the type of player you would always want on your side. Mind you, Colin surprised me and showed us all a side to him we never knew existed when we met up in Sydney for a special Wallabies fund-raising evening a few years ago. To see Colin Meads singing Elvis Presley songs, and singing them very well, too, was something else.

A couple of South Africans I encountered during my time in the game, I'd have also liked on my side. I am sure they would find places today. Jan Ellis and Piet Greyling were flank forwards; both were tremendously competitive, strong players and were part of some outstanding South African back rows in their era. I thought of them again in late 1998 when I was watching the South African tourists on their Britain and Ireland visit. During the course of that tour, a very talented young flank forward began to emerge in their Test side, Bobby Skinstad, and set me thinking about Ellis and Greyling.

Greyling was a fabulous forward, and I don't use that word lightly. He was a hunter of the loose ball and the ball carrier, quick to the breakdown and powerful in the tackle. He could rip the ball off men bigger than himself. Ellis was also hugely talented, extremely quick and devastating in the tackle. It was Jan Ellis's powerful tackle early in the first Test between South Africa and the 1968 British Lions, in Pretoria, that abruptly finished Barry John's tour. Barry broke his collar bone as he was thrown on to the hard ground by Ellis's tackle.

Another great former Springbok international whom I have got to know well in more recent years is Jannie Engelbrecht. He represented South Africa from 1960 to 1969. Jannie now runs his own vineyard in the hills just outside Stellenbosch, a short drive out of Cape Town, and he makes some wonderful red wines under the name 'Rust En Vrede'. The setting is quite magnificent. His home is one of the original houses built by the early Dutch settlers in the second half of the seventeenth century, and his modern winery is right alongside it. There is a vast lawn and a swimming pool, all set against a backdrop of the vineyards with rolling hills behind. I have been there on a few occasions and had a wonderful time on each visit.

When I think back to the type of rugby those South Africans played, I feel that they were performing the modern type of game thirty years ago. They were very tough and strong, driving hard in the loose and supporting constantly, making powerful tackles all over the field. Most of them were very comfortable with the ball in their hands, especially the third member of that excellent back row unit, No. 8 Tommy Bedford. He was a superb ball player with all the skills. I suppose today, some South Africans would think Tommy Bedford too small to play the modern game, but if ball skills are your yardstick, I'd say he would have been sure to win a place in a modern-day side.

At this time, there is something of a dearth of great No. 8s. I mean powerful, hard, foraging forwards with the drive and determination to dog it out with their pack, but also men with the ball skills and pace to excel at the highest level. Only the very best possess that combination. Over the years, a few worthy candidates spring to mind. Tommy Bedford and Morne du Plessis from South Africa would be ideal candidates, Mervyn Davies and Alan Pask, both of Wales and the British Lions, are very definitely two others. Then there would be those two outstanding New Zealanders, Brian Lochore and Wayne Shelford, All Blacks who were among the finest exponents of the No. 8's art in their time. Ken Goodall of Ireland was another superbly talented player.

What intrigues me most concerning this subject is not whether all these players would have made it in the modern game, but how much better would they have been as professional rugby players, training and preparing each day for their next match?

The modern-day player has an enormous advantage. He can spend hours on the training ground each day, working on his fitness and skills. When he suffers an injury, he receives the finest medical care money can buy, and when he isn't training or playing, he can rest, either sitting at home relaxing or sleeping. That latter aspect, remember, is just as much a part of the professional sportsman's schedule as his work on the training ground. I remember hearing about Alan Jones, that shrewd, articulate manager of the 1984 Australian Wallabies on their tour of Britain and Ireland, answering a question about where a certain player was one afternoon.

'He's training, mate.'

'But you finished training at lunchtime,' was the retort. 'It's four o'clock.'

'He's still training – he's in bed asleep,' quipped Jones.

How right he was. Rest and recuperation is an integral part of the top-class sportsman's preparation. How many players from years gone by could afford that luxury? Even their training had to be fitted in among work schedules and family commitments.

What sort of physical condition might J.P.R. Williams, for example, have attained, had he not been working on his medical studies while he was playing top-class rugby for London Welsh, Wales and the British Lions? Imagine if Williams had had the chance of regular quality training time during the day, not the rushed hour or two after a day's work when the body is tired and drained. It's some thought, isn't it?

There were plenty of other fine players I knew who would also have benefited enormously from professional training. Roger Uttley, a fine England back row forward, suffered from back trouble for much of his career and might have been able to solve it and get even fitter under professional preparation. The Lions selectors recognised Uttley's all-round footballing skills by playing him as a flanker in the Test matches on the 1974 tour of South Africa, even though he'd been chosen as a second row forward.

Peter Dixon, an excellent England and British Lions back row man from the early 1970s, would have flourished in the modern game. Dixon went on that memorable 1971 Lions tour as an uncapped player and worked his way into the Test team, an outstanding achievement given the quality of players in competition for the place. Dixon was a highly intelligent forward and a splendid ball handler. Fran Cotton was another great England forward of that era, a big yet mobile man in the front row.

Maybe all the English players of my time suffered from the same general malaise – a less than focused approach from those at the top. What happened to us at Cardiff one day when we went to London to meet Harlequins in a club match spoke volumes for the state of English rugby around that time.

We'd been told we would play the match on the main RFU ground at Twickenham, which Harlequins used to use for most of their major club games and continued to use for a while even after The Stoop had been developed. It was a vast cavernous ground at the best of times but for a club game, it seemed enormous. Nevertheless, we always got a buzz out of playing at Twickenham. We rolled up there this particular day with a team filled with internationals, only to be told that someone else needed the ground that afternoon; there had been a mix-up on the fixture card. So we said, 'Oh well, that's not a problem, boys, we'll play on The Stoop.' We all trooped over the A316 only to find that some team was already playing a match on the main pitch. So the first teams of Harlequins and Cardiff ended up having to go around the ground asking anyone who had parked their cars on the back pitch at The Stoop, the thirds pitch, please to move them because we wanted to play our game there.

Perhaps John Bevan of Wales would have been one of the most successful players in today's game. Strong, sturdy, thoroughly combative and determined, he was a wing who accepted the physical nature of the game with relish and was as strong as an ox. Maybe, too, the former England scrum-half Steve Smith would have become an even greater player under the demands of professionalism. If he'd been around today and had knuckled down to professionalism's demands, he could have been a fantastic player because he was strong and fast.

One player who was tailor-made for the modern game was Barry Llewelyn, the former Newport, Llanelli and Wales front row forward. Barry played only three seasons of international rugby – 1970, 1971 and 1972 – but he was a wonderful player: fast, mobile and a great footballer. John Lloyd, the Bridgend and Wales prop forward was a bit small by the standards of most prop forwards in those days but he was a great Sevens player and also a wonderful footballer. While on the subject of

Welsh props, what of Graham Price – he would have been an obvious candidate for the modern-day game because as well as being a tremendous scrummager, he got around the field so well.

Another Welshman who would have been a superstar today was my old half-back colleague, Phil Bennett, although he might have had to be a bit more switched on with his timing and arrangements off the rugby field. I'll never forget the time we went to Paris for a match against France. Well, on the Saturday night of course, you hardly ever went to bed. You'd attend the banquet, then you'd be off into the night with the French boys, partying and celebrating. By the time you had finished, it was around six or seven o'clock in the morning and it wasn't worth going to bed, because bags would have to be down in the hotel reception by eight. There would just be time for breakfast before you climbed on to the bus for the airport.

On this particular occasion, we got out to Charles de Gaulle airport, which I think we were using for the first time. We were all booked on a British Airways flight direct to Cardiff. I remember going for a stroll with Gerald Davies after we'd checked in, but neither of us had a clue where we were or where we were supposed to be going. More by luck than judgement, we suddenly saw the correct satellite where our plane was parked. As we walked up to it, the stewardess said, 'Hurry up, please, we are about to shut the doors.' Well, Gerald and I knew that most of the players had checked in behind us and couldn't possibly have got up there and boarded the plane. We told them, but the airline staff just said, 'We're sorry, we have a slot for take-off and we're going.' All the committee were in their seats when Gerald and I boarded the plane but there were rows and rows of empty seats where the players should have been. We took off and flew home. When we walked into the arrivals hall at Cardiff airport, all the wives of the boys were waiting. 'Where's Phil? Where's John?' they said. Over half the squad had been left back in Paris. They had the devil's own job getting another plane home. In the end, I think some didn't get back to Cardiff until around midnight on the Sunday.

The French had some superb players who would have made their mark on the present-day game, most notably, Jean Pierre Rives, Jerome Gallion, a scrum-half who was always dangerous breaking from the base of the scrum, and Jean Claude Skrela, now the coach of France.

Jean Pierre, the old fox, took me out after one match in Paris which Wales had lost, and we had a marvellous night together. Jean Pierre rarely drank anything other than bottled French water but on this night, he did have some drinks – wine, champagne, brandy perhaps. We were in a taxi crossing Paris at a very late hour, when I remember Jean Pierre awakening and calling out for the cab to stop at once. I knew why, I'd known the feeling a few times! Anyway, we pulled up in a fairly busy street and stumbled out on to the pathway where Jean Pierre was promptly sick, very nearly at the feet of three astonished Welsh fans who had seen the cab pull up abruptly and two dinner-jacketed gentlemen emerge. They looked at Jean Pierre, looked at me and said, 'Well done, Gareth, bach – we might have lost the match, but we've beaten them fair and square in the drinking, boyo!'

As for the great teams, I saw plenty during my career. Whether it was on the international field with Wales or the British Lions, playing for my club Cardiff or for Cardiff College of Education or, going back still further, Millfield School, there were always sides who caught the eye. It may seem an indulgence to include some teams I played for myself, but it would be hard to leave out the 1971 British Lions, for instance, now destined forever to be remembered as the only Lions touring squad to win a Test series in New Zealand in the twentieth century.

I was twelve years old when I first saw a touring side play in Wales. The memory of it, very nearly forty years later, remains strong. The 1961 South Africans were captained by Avril Malan and became a mighty team. They had some wonderful players and went home with a proud record. In the British Isles and France, they played a total of thirty-four matches winning thirty-one, drawing two and losing just once, 6–0 to the Barbarians in Cardiff, in their final match on British soil. John Gainsford, Jannie Engelbrecht, Keith Oxlee, Johaan Claasen and Doug Hopwood were outstanding performers and another Springbok, who was to become one of the world's great locks, Frik du Preez, made his international debut on that tour. On 29 October, I saw them beat Cardiff at the Arms Park by two goals and a penalty goal (13 points) to nil. Their size, speed and strength deeply impressed me. To tour Britain and then France and lose only one match, was an immense record.

Six years later, I faced a touring team at Cardiff, the 1967 New Zealand All Blacks. In between, Wilson Whineray brought over the New Zealanders in 1963–4 and they too, like the '61 'Boks, had a marvellous record: thirty-two wins from thirty-four matches, one drawn, one lost. Those All Blacks played much more of a ten-man game. It was typical New Zealand stuff of that era – hard, driving forwards, exceptional strength and durability at half-back and to back it all up, the goal-kicking of the phenomenal Don Clarke. It was highly successful if somewhat dour.

The '67 All Blacks, too, had some great players – Brian Lochore, the captain, Colin Meads and Kel Tremain among the forwards and outside them Chris Laidlaw and Earl Kirton at half-back, Ian MacRae and Malcolm Dick in the three-quarters with Fergie McCormick at full-back. They played a different game of rugby from previous All Black teams. They had the usual strong pack of forwards but with a big, fast, mobile back row. They had backs who could use the ball and possessed real pace. Of the fifteen matches they played in Britain, they won fourteen and drew one. That draw, 3–3, was against an East Wales side which was captained for the day by one G.O. Edwards. The match should have been played on a Saturday but heavy snow forced its postponement until the following Wednesday. Thirty-five thousand people turned up at the Arms Park to see it and East Wales played some outstanding rugby. We played them off the park for most of the match and what a cracking game it turned out to be.

East Wales had a fair side out, including players who would become or already were established internationals, such as the Cardiff backs Keri Jones, Gerald Davies, Barry John and myself plus the likes of Tess O'Shea, Jeff Young, 'Boyo' James, John Hickey, Tony Gray and Ron Jones up front. Frank Wilson scored a twenty-second minute try for us when he was first to reach a drop goal attempt by Barry John that went wide.

Unfortunately, between us, David Griffiths (brother of the great Gareth Griffiths, a British Lions and Wales full-back and wing of the 1950s and our full-back that day), and I missed four penalty kicks. It was to prove costly. Ten minutes from the end, Tony Steel got the ball forty yards from our line, beat Keri Jones, Davies and Griffiths on a strong run and made it into the left corner. Fergie McCormick's conversion just missed but we had been pegged back, when we ought to have been clear. Barry John's attempted drop goal in the final minute sailed inches wide.

Fred Allen and Charlie Saxton, the All Blacks management duo, said they would have had no problems accepting defeat on the day. They confessed they had been lucky not to lose. Fred Allen was their guru, a man who had got them playing in a more expansive fashion. They would pull you first this way then that across the field.

Three days later at Twickenham, Keri Jones, Gerald Davies, Barry John and myself ran out to face New Zealand once again, this time for the Barbarians in the tourists' final match. For Keri, Barry and me it was the third time we played them on the tour, for we'd all been in the Welsh national side beaten 13–6 in Cardiff. That match was typical of games against New Zealand teams – we made one mistake and it cost us the game. But we had missed chances that could have turned the game, too. The Barbarians actually led 6–3 going into injury time, although we weren't quite sure how. The All Blacks had dominated possession but we'd held on, snatching a try by the English centre Bob Lloyd and kicking a penalty, by Scotland's full-back Stewart Wilson. The match turned in the final minutes because this was yet another New Zealand side that never knew the meaning of the word defeat. By the end, they had won 13–6 with two tries, by Ian MacRae and Tony Steel.

You had to respect their verve and durability in finishing like that at the end of such a hard tour. I have always held a deep respect for the way that particular New Zealand touring squad played the game. They showed that All Black teams could progress from just a forward driving game based on little other than ferocious power up front and outstanding goal-kicking. I was only twenty but I had learned all about the qualities required to play against the New Zealanders and their refusal to give up under any circumstances. I became a great admirer of their commitment and self-belief and those lessons remained with me throughout my entire playing career.

At the start of the 1970s, the British Lions put together a touring party which some argue remains the finest they have ever sent overseas. That may or may not be the case and it is a hypothetical argument. The strength of the opposition is a major factor to be taken into account in determining the truth of such a claim, and that is a variable. I have mentioned the merits of that Lions squad elsewhere in this book. There was tons of raw talent, backed up by superb coaching from Carwyn James, a man who didn't fill your head with complicated moves and theory but drew the very best out of his players with a few well-chosen words. What was also demonstrated by that Lions party was considerable character. We lost both our likely Test props in the Canterbury match shortly before the first Test, but in the face of adversity, we came through to victory with courage and determination.

There was an air of invincibility about New Zealand and South Africa in their own backyard and somehow we had to come to terms with that. It helped to have decision-makers throughout the team, guys who could improvise and play off the cuff. Behind it all, there was Carwyn, giving us the freedom to play.

People in the modern game talk about the value of counter-attacking by the so-called back three unit – the combination of left and right wings, plus the full-back. We were doing that more than twenty years ago on that Lions tour and the one that followed. We could do it because we had excellent footballers who were all comfortable with the ball in their hands.

Following that successful 1971 Lions team, I would nominate any one of the Welsh teams that won a total of three Grand Slams, five Triple Crowns and five international championship titles from 1971 to 1979. I consider myself richly blessed to have been a part of it all. There were changes in the team during the course of those nine seasons, but a core of players survived through most of the decade which meant the team retained a solid base of consistency and experience. That was certainly a critical factor in what we achieved.

Another factor that made us different from, say, the English teams of that time and subsequent eras, was that we had players who could improvise so well on the field. Thirteen of the Welsh side that began the 1970s went on the 1971 Lions tour to New Zealand. Only Dai Morris, the flanker who hated travelling so much, didn't go and they said that was because he was too small. He should have gone, he would have been superb. Rugby was simpler in those days, we just played with a little top-up assistance from the coach. There was never any rigid plan, no thumping the table in preparation to make sure we knew exactly what we were going to do before we even went out. Perhaps that was what made us special – even we didn't quite know what was coming.

We also had a good strong pack of forwards available in that decade – Delme Thomas, John Lloyd, Mervyn Davies, Geoff Evans, Mike Roberts, Jeff Young. Lots of power there. But it was probably the way we played that made it so special, with plenty of footballing quality and a lovely style.

In 1984, an Australian team touring the British Isles won against all four countries for the first time. But then, the '84 Wallabies, coached by Alan Jones, captained by Andrew Slack and so inspired by Mark Ella, really were an exceptional team. Not even the likes of Michael Hawker, an outstandingly talented centre who had already won twenty-four caps, could force his way into the Test team on that tour.

The Australians arrived with a young scrum-half in their ranks who had yet to play in a Test match, but Nick Farr-Jones came through on the tour, made the Test spot his own and was destined to become one of the world's great scrum-halves of his time. Outside him, Ella played perhaps the finest rugby of his life, scoring a try in every one of the four Test matches as Australia beat England, Wales, Ireland and Scotland for their historic 'Grand Slam'.

David Campese and Mark Ella, who were later to come together in Italian rugby, were great performers, entertainers and try scorers. Their innovative play, their creative genius, seemed to epitomise those Wallabies. Supplementing the footballing skills of Ella, Campese, Farr-Jones and their strong full-back Roger Gould, was the forward power of Simon Poidevin, Steve Cutler and Steve Tuynman. Then there was 'Topo' Rodriguez, the Argentine who had emigrated to Australia and qualified as a Wallaby. His scrummaging was immense, as the famous pushover try against Wales at Cardiff illustrated. It was a key moment in the entire tour.

They were a fine all-round side that played superb, counterattacking football which delighted audiences everywhere they went. They also had a supreme motivator in Jones, a clever man who seemed able to charm the media with some witty and telling phrases.

It is much more important to have a great side than a great coach. Superb coaches should always extract the maximum possible from the talent within their ranks. Without good players, not even the finest coach can produce match winners behind the scrum or forwards able to dominate possession. Good or even great coaches should have an impact on good teams, but it isn't always so. I feel that England have been a good side at certain times in recent years despite the coaches they have had. I am thinking of that hugely powerful England side of the early 1990s which was pushing aside just about every team they met. They were a great side, and with Jeremy Guscott and Rory Underwood behind the scrum, they had potentially exciting match winners. Yet they played boring rugby and it seemed such a waste of all that hard-won possession. I wonder what that side might have achieved under the influence of someone like Nick Mallett of South Africa or John Hart of New Zealand, someone able to give them a vision of the fifteen-man game and how it can both entertain and succeed. It is a fascinating thought.

When you can combine the two, a fine team and a great coach, it is a rare and special mixture and that is what those 1984 Wallabies had.

Really top notch, world-class teams rarely come along like buses, five or six in a row. The best rugby teams, those you would choose as the very best of the century, occur only occasionally. But the side the New Zealand All Blacks put together in 1995 certainly merits categorisation as great.

They did not win the World Cup that year in South Africa, losing in extra time of a dramatic final, but they were still the outstanding team of that tournament, a superb side bursting with talent, power and creative thinking. There was the hard core of experience epitomised by players such as Sean Fitzpatrick, Michael Brewer, Ian Jones, Zinzan Brooke, Walter Little and Frank Bunce. Then there was the more youthful element of Jeff

Wilson, Andrew Mehrtens, Jonah Lomu and Josh Kronfeld. It was a tremendous combination and they played some marvellous rugby throughout the tournament. By rights, they should have become world champions, just to show some tangible reward for all their fine rugby. South Africa's determined resistance in the final denied them but no one can take away from those All Blacks their right to inclusion among the best. They had done well in southern hemisphere contests for some time, and played scintillating rugby at every stage of the World Cup, apart from the final. But I do not believe one ordinary match ruins a great side's reputation.

South Africa's defence that day was superb and the emotion of the occasion clearly helped them. But for sheer quality and class and for the fine football they had played through the tournament, the New Zealanders were the better team in every respect except the result. Bunce and Little were strong centres, clever tactically, aware of opportunities and how to utilise them. When I talk of players thinking on their feet and making decisions on the hoof, those two come to mind. Robin Brooke and Ian Jones were a formidable second row pairing; agile, good in the line-outs and strong. Behind them, there was the pure pace of Kronfeld, the wily experience of Zinzan at No. 8 and Michael Brewer's rugged competitiveness on the blindside flank. The front row of Olo Brown, 'Fitzie' and Craig Dowd was solid and uncompromising and the half-backs behind them, Graeme Bachop and Mehrtens, were quick and positive. The so-called 'spine' of the team, that imaginary line which runs through a side starting at hooker (Fitzpatrick) to lock (Jones) to No. 8 (Brooke) and then from fly-half (Mehrtens) to inside-centre (Bunce) and full-back (Osborne), was very strong.

Today, the All Blacks again have marvellous performers in

most of those key positions: Christian Cullen or Jeff Wilson at full-back, Mehrtens still at outside-half, the superbly talented and strong Justin Marshall at scrum-half and a host of others competing for the positions among the forwards. Bad New Zealand teams are rarities.

All in all, it should have added up to a World Cup-winning squad. Perhaps that's the true appeal of rugby – even when the best go out to play, they're never certain of victory.

In the years of isolation when South African sport paid for its government's apartheid policy, a couple of outstanding performers played probably their best rugby. Danie Gerber and Naas Botha were exceptional players, both of whom are still idolised in their country today, long after their retirement. You won't find Gerber or Botha in the list of leading cap winners in South African rugby because, although their Test match careers both started in 1980 and ended in 1992, they won only a handful of caps, Botha twenty-eight, Gerber twenty-four. The years of isolation were as cruel to them as they were to another hugely talented South African sportsman, the great cricketer Barry Richards.

We saw too few glimpses of their talents. Gerber would probably have become as well known as Jonah Lomu had he been around today, a strong, big, fast centre who was devilishly hard to stop in full flight. If the 1995 World Cup catapulted Lomu into the spotlight, Gerber would have enjoyed a similar impact a decade earlier, had there been a World Cup then and had South Africa been involved.

Naas Botha was a remarkable outside-half. He had the kicking ability of the best from more recent eras – Grant Fox, Michael Lynagh or Neil Jenkins. I played against him in 1977 when he was eighteen and I was in a World XV which went to

South Africa for a series of games. I remember putting pressure on him well inside his own 25 only for him to rifle the ball down to our own 25 with hardly any effort at all, leaving me staggered. I knew full well that the ball flew further at altitude in South Africa, but it was still a phenomenal kick. He showed lots of footballing qualities but it was only right at the end of his career, when he was past his best, that he reappeared in sanctioned Test match rugby. It was his great misfortune to be around at that difficult time for rugby in his country.

There is an amusing story about Naas which is widely told in South Africa. Naas was known as a player who usually dictated the course of a match by his decision-making and selection of options in the No. 10 shirt. Put it another way, his centres may not always have seen as much of the ball as they might have liked. One day, Naas played in an important match and later that evening, went to the airport to fly home. As he settled into his seat on the aircraft, he was bothered by only one thing – the man next to him kept looking at him intently. Naas put up with it for a while and then decided a personal introduction was the right approach.

'You probably know who I am. I'm Naas Botha, the famous rugby player,' he said to the stranger.

'You probably should know who I am, I'm so-and-so, and I'm also a rugby player,' the man replied.

Naas smiled. 'Really, is that so. And who do you play for?'

'I play in your team and I'm the poor devil who is a centre outside you!'

Maybe because I was a scrum-half, I always saw the best qualities of Naas Botha. And I wouldn't have minded having him as a half-back partner.

But what of some other great players from the 1980s, players

165

who stirred the emotion with the quality of their play? In New Zealand, I think of John Kirwan, a wonderfully powerful, fast wing who was so outstanding in the 1987 World Cup. Then, like all players who appeared in a particular position, I think of those who might have been my opponents in another era – David Kirk and Dave Loveridge, two fine All Black scrum-halves. Kirk was a cracking scrum-half, a player I always admired. He was fast, incisive, a lovely match player. Loveridge was a classic New Zealand half-back; a player with a solid basic game who linked extremely well with his back row.

I have always enjoyed watching the skills of scrum-halves from around the world. Kirk, Loveridge, Farr-Jones, Going, Howley, Gregan, Van der Westhuizen . . . whoever they are, it is always a privilege to sit back and admire their skills. South Africa's Joost van der Westhuizen is an outstanding footballer with an exceptional strike rate, and his speed off the mark and ability to demolish any defence are without peer. He suits the modern game perfectly because, with back row forwards having to remain bound in to the scrum until the ball has gone, he is allowed those extra few seconds that a player of his great pace can exploit so well.

Although Joost is susceptible to losing his poise at times, particularly when he is under pressure, and his passing can become a little erratic, he remains a consummate performer. He is, in my judgement, the best No. 9 in the world although Justin Marshall is probably the most technically proficient scrum-half. He is extremely astute, reads the game well and is a very good tactician and excellent kicker. Robert Howley of Wales is getting into that category. He is very quick and both his kicking and tactical appreciation are improving all the time.

As for George Gregan, the Australian, he is a nuggety little half-back, a scrum-half who loves to dog it out with the best. He's a terrier of a player, never happier than when he is hammering away through or with his forwards, or securing ball for his outside-half. George also has the priceless knack of so often being in the right place at the right time, whether it be for a tackle or a try-scoring opportunity.

Another who deserves a mention is the French scrum-half Philippe Carbonneau, a player quick enough to have played centre for the French club Stade Toulouse and also for France. Like all the others, Philippe is a real handful for a defence. If you have a scrum-half who needs several defenders to keep an eye on him, you have a real asset in the team. All these players are supreme performers, all different in their styles of play.

I love watching Jeremy Guscott play, but I detect a sense of frustration he has probably felt for much of his career. He has played a lot of games with his hands in his pockets waiting for the pass or opportunity. Every so often, he reminds us of his real talent and when he does, it is a special moment. Will Carling, his partner at centre for so long in the England team, was a good, solid player, but there weren't too many occasions when he made me jump out of my seat. Jerry Guscott does.

We have seen some fabulous players over recent years. In no particular order, what about the try-scoring genius of Ieuan Evans, the power, pace and skills of Philippe Sella, the quiet authority of Michael Lynagh and the strength and threat of Gavin Hastings? Before Gavin in the Scottish side, I always admired the skills of those talented half-backs John Rutherford and Roy Laidlaw. Then there was Ollie Campbell of Ireland, a true match-winner and one of the nicest men you could ever wish to meet. Jim Renwick and Colin Deans were other Scots for whom I always held a deep admiration and what of the mercurial skills of the great Serge Blanco in the French team? I'll never forget the first time I heard his name mentioned. I was driving home one night at the end of the 1970s when a reporter came on the radio with details of the Wales B match against France B that night. If the name Blanco was used once, it must have been repeated half a dozen times, such were his stirring deeds. The reporter prophesied great things for this exciting young French full-back and Serge went on to justify all the expectations. He became one of the greatest players the game has ever known.

I respected several Englishmen from their highly successful era of the late 1980s, early 1990s. Chief among them were Rory Underwood, Rob Andrew and Dean Richards. Rory had an outstanding record, and so too in a different way did Rob Andrew who was so instrumental in guiding England to their Grand Slams and Triple Crowns of that period.

As for Dean Richards, I don't think England ever fully appreciated his enormous talents until he was dropped. Without him, they quickly came to realise his great value. I sat with Dean one day at Twickenham before an England match for which he had not been selected, and he was so despondent at being left out. I had no TV commitments that day and we had a long chat. I tried to encourage him, told him his chance would come again and urged him to keep going. Dean was no greyhound as a No. 8 but he suited the English approach, based on control and efficiency, to a tee. Had he played in the 1991 World Cup final against Australia, I am sure England would have become World Champions that day.

It has been my privilege and my pleasure to see all these

fine players grace so many of the international rugby fields of the world. Comparisons between eras are largely speculative; so much changes from each generation to the next. I've enjoyed watching them and am grateful for a fund of great memories.

CHAPTER EIGHT

The 1999 World Cup

It has been called the biggest white elephant in the history of the world, a scandalous waste of money, a legacy to lunacy, and a lot worse besides. Undeniably, it has cost an absolute fortune and all the banging and hammering which has been needed twenty-four hours a day since last autumn has probably wrecked the sleep pattern of countless city centre residents. Nevertheless, the Millennium Stadium stands resplendent as a permanent feature of the Cardiff skyline. I, for one, am pleased to see it. All Wales has something of which it can collectively feel proud.

Take my word for it, if you knew the old Cardiff ground, you would look at this magnificent new stadium and be grateful for the wonderful new creation that has risen in its place. Going back some years, Cardiff's pitch would have had twenty matches played on it by Christmas, plus training on it twice a week, and the surface would have been like a bog by January, just in time for the Five Nations Championship. It's easy to forget those days, but we shouldn't. This super new stadium is one of the finest in world sport.

The argument over its location rumbled on for too long. A greenfield site near Bridgend? Please, be serious. Why build one of the world's great stadia in the middle of nowhere (even though it would have been most convenient from a personal point of view since I live near Bridgend)? It always had to be in Cardiff. The home of Welsh rugby is a dream location, right in the middle of the capital city. It's like having Twickenham just off Oxford Circus or Eden Park at the back of Queen Street, in Auckland. There's no travelling out into the provinces by public transport, cramming on to trains or sitting in long traffic jams; just the beautiful convenience of city centre restaurants, cafés and pubs and a short stroll to the ground. Ideal!

There might not be as much parking space provided as you'd expect at a new greenfield site like, for example, the new Madejski Stadium at Reading, but not so much is needed in a city centre location. Buses pass the front gate and the main railway station is just across the road. I'm sure there will be room nearby for Tom Jones to land his helicopter when he flies in from the States! What else do you need? To my mind, that is one of the reasons why it is so good. If you come from Swansea or Newport for a Welsh match, take the train – you don't need a car.

Wherever you go in the world, people know about Cardiff Arms Park. They remember the great moments, the glorious tries, the big events. How could we have moved our spiritual home steeped in so much history to a green field somewhere in the country near Bridgend? In my opinion, Cardiff was always the only serious location.

What encourages me most is the expectation that it will be a national stadium, not just for rugby. The cost of building it has been approximately £120 million, of which the Millennium Commission provided around £60 million. That sounds a fortune but I am willing to bet that ten years down the road, it will seem a modest enough sum. But you have got to service that debt and six games of World Cup rugby won't do that. It has to be run as a business. I hope it will be used for all kinds of events and special happenings. Imagine hearing a great opera star or a famous rock band giving a concert there. I'm sure it will become a symbol of Wales which everyone will welcome.

What of the World Cup itself, the tournament into which so much money and effort has been poured? The formbook suggests that this World Cup may not be as clear-cut as the previous tournaments. Of course, you still wouldn't stray from the big three, South Africa, the holders, New Zealand and Australia, to predict the eventual winners. But, on the form England have displayed at varying times over the last year, I would say you have to add them to the group from which the winners will emerge. Two factors are in England's favour, and France's, too. Firstly, the tournament is being held in the northern hemisphere, for only the second time. The last time, 1991, England reached the final. The stadia (except of course the new one in Cardiff) will be more familiar to them than to the southern hemisphere teams; there will be a feeling of being at home for most of the competition; they will be used to the weather conditions at that time of the year and the soft grounds are something they grew up with. All those factors count, maybe not adding up to a massive advantage, but an advantage all the same.

Secondly, the tournament starts on 1 October and runs until the 6 November, right at the end of the southern hemisphere's rugby year. Their top players will have been in training since early January, they will have had top-level opposition starting with the Super 12 tournament from February and will either have been playing, training or thinking rugby right up to October. I think that could be a crucial factor. You only have to look at the evidence of South Africa's tour of Britain and Ireland last autumn to see what effect fatigue, both mental and physical, can have on players. They were weary and it affected their form. It may not be very different by the time the World Cup starts. They will have had Super 12 and Tri-Nations rugby for months and every game in those competitions is akin to a Test match.

The last eighteen months in world rugby have proved that even the best rugby nations are vulnerable. Leaving aside South Africa, who would have thought New Zealand would have lost five consecutive Test matches last year? That was simply unthinkable, a disastrous run by their elevated standards.

I believe you have to take England seriously. Any team that has got its defensive formations right and is able to withstand sustained pressure has to be an equal bet for victory in a match, whatever the opposition. One of the southern hemisphere nations will doubtless start the tournament as favourites. England will feel they have it all to do, everything to prove, and will be determined to make the most of their chance.

France, I am sure, will feel the same way. They so nearly beat South Africa in the semi-final in Durban in 1995 and you only have to run through their team to see the power, quality and pace at their disposal to know they pose a threat. There has never been much doubt about the power of a French pack, and behind them, there is real pace and craft, talent which can open up a defence. Unarguably, we did not see the best of the French in the 1999 Five Nations Championship. They looked off the pace, unsettled as a team partly due to so many injuries, and had several players operating below their best. But the French have the capacity to bounce back quicker than anyone.

Look at the quality of their three-quarters. Thomas Castaignede is one of the most exciting players in the modern game, a quick, visionary player who can open up opponents from the outside-half position. Outside him, there are hugely skilful players available at centre such as Stephane Glas, although he broke a leg just before the 1999 Five Nations Championship, Christophe Lamaison, Franck Comba, Richard Dourthe and others. Then you have some seriously quick wings; Philippe Bernat-Salles is as fast as anyone I can remember, and there is also Thomas Lombard, Xavier Garbajosa and Christophe Dominici. Full-back Emile N'Tamack scored an outstanding hat-trick of tries in the match against Wales in Paris in March 1999.

French rugby always seems capable of producing new players whenever they are needed, who perform most creditably on the international stage. I think the French present a danger to anyone on any day. You never quite know whether they will be up for it, but underestimate them and they will punish you. They have the capacity to take a side completely apart if they start to play.

There could be another factor in France's favour. Their soccer team lifted the World Cup last year in memorable style; what an incentive it will surely be to their rugby team to try and emulate that feat. Imagine one nation holding both the soccer and rugby World Cups simultaneously. It would be a unique achievement. If the French are not motivated by that thought, they won't be motivated by anything.

If you look at the draw, I feel France have a clear advantage.

On paper (although I know rugby isn't played very often on that surface!) it appears likely that the French will meet Ireland in the quarter-final. If that happens, you would have to give them a pretty reasonable chance of getting through, although given the way the Ireland–France Five Nations match went at the start of the 1999 Championship, perhaps you would not bet on it. Upsets can happen. Once a side reaches any semi-final, they all have a good chance. France have reached a World Cup final before, in 1987. They know what is required to go all the way. They got as far as the quarter-finals in 1991 but four years later could well have won that semi-final in Durban.

As for England, so much looks like depending on their Pool B match against New Zealand, a game which could be very close. If they lose that, the likelihood is that they will have to take on South Africa in Paris in the quarter-finals and getting past them could be a tough task. But if England were to beat the All Blacks, their path to the final might be less intimidating. They might have to face France in the semi-final, and what a tremendous match that would be. Both semis will be played at Twickenham, which would be a major advantage to England.

It is my fervent hope that some of the other competing nations, such as Wales and Scotland, will provide some upsets, whatever the opposition. I was greatly encouraged by Wales's progress once Graham Henry arrived from Auckland to take charge of the national side, and I think we showed in our internationals last season what is possible from this Welsh team. The defeat in Scotland at the start of 1999 in the Five Nations opener was disappointing and the loss to Ireland at Wembley which followed made things look bleak. But the second half of that Championship and then the summer proved that Wales do have fine players; Henry's task is to mould them into a real team, with plenty of self-belief. The first signs that that might be happening came with victory over France in Paris. To win there, for the first time since 1975, was a wonderful achievement, an uplifting, proud moment for all of Welsh rugby. To do it in such style, especially in the first forty minutes, and hold their nerve for that 34–33 win, demonstrated what might be possible for Wales in the World Cup.

If that progress can be maintained, I see no reason why Wales cannot produce an upset or two that challenges the established order. That would be good, not just for rugby in Wales but throughout the world. It would show other nations, such as the Italians who came so close to beating England in a World Cup qualifying match in 1998, just what can be achieved.

I hope it won't be a World Cup dominated by defences. What I would like to see emerge from this tournament is a game that is attractive to millions of kids throughout the world. Whether those of us in rugby like to fool ourselves or not, this game still does not compare with football in terms of world appeal. It will take many years, perhaps even decades or generations, to close that gap significantly. But if this World Cup leaves kids who watch it saying, 'I want to play that game,' it will have been a success, no matter who eventually wins it.

However, every World Cup to date has proved to be a watershed for major changes in the game and if this one is the same, please let us have some thought from the powers that be before changing direction in the structure of our game. For example, what do we do about the smaller nations? What is the best way to encourage and assist their development? How shall we integrate them into the family of rugby without creating the one-sided slaughters like some in the qualifying tournament for this World Cup?

We are kidding ourselves if we pretend that any more than a handful of nations play this game seriously. Rugby union might be played in more than a hundred countries but the reality is that it's only performed at a reasonable level in a few. I want to see a definite increase in the number of nations playing the game to a high standard. I suppose there is a view that until you play against the stronger nations, you won't know how good or bad you are and you won't improve. The problem of the smaller rugby nations is not an easy one to solve. If you bring them to the finals of the World Cup to play in a Plate competition against countries of roughly similar strength, as some have suggested, isn't there a danger that they will forever be playing in Plate competitions, never against the big boys?

Not too long ago, I went to Japan to help them promote a Japanese Sevens tournament. I discovered genuine concerns among rugby people there that after their 145-point defeat by New Zealand in the 1995 World Cup, there was no longer a place for Japan in world rugby. My reaction to that was, 'Don't be so silly, of course there is.' They were wondering whether they should concentrate just on Sevens but I told them they would be wrong to do that. Japan have proved over many years they have the ability to be a member of the world game at a good level; technically, they are very good. I remember after one Welsh match against them our hooker, Bobby Windsor, telling me it was one of the toughest games he'd ever played.

My overall feeling is that you have got to give these countries competition so that they can measure their standards and their progress. There is no doubt there is a disparity between the top ten nations in the world and the rest. But, while being aware of mis-matches, we should still encourage competition.

Another aspect of the World Cup which was in the headlines

late last year was the question of ticket prices for these finals. It's true that a ticket price of £100, never mind the £150 and even £250 mentioned for some seats at the final itself, robs the man in the street of the chance to attend matches, certainly with his family. Few in Wales have that sort of loose change in their pockets. But that has been the case for the last few years in top-line sport. Prices for the soccer World Cup finals in France last year were expensive, and desperately difficult to come by. With corporate business dominating most sporting arenas especially for the big events nowadays, isn't that the way of the world? I don't say I approve of it but it's a fact of life, and I have to admit to being part of it.

I do not see an answer to it. These huge competitions cost enormous amounts of money to organise. Facilities are massively expensive. The World Cup is expected to gross in the region of £115 million, with net profits of around £50 million, which demonstrates the cost of running and administering the event. The tournament that began life eleven years ago as something of a fun competition which took place almost without people knowing what was going on, has become a massive affair, one of the highlights of the sporting calendar. As rugby men, we should be proud of that, proud of its enormous growth in the course of a single decade.

I understand the unease of those who see the game marching off into the arms of the corporate business world, with many lifelong followers struggling to keep in touch. But I must say I am hugely looking forward to this event and am convinced it will be great for Wales. The last World Cup in the northern hemisphere produced some outstanding characters and players – David Campese, John Kirwan, Serge Blanco, Nick Farr-Jones, Jeremy Guscott and many more. There were marvellous matches, too. Who can forget Ireland's compelling clash with Australia at Lansdowne Road when the eventual champions were within two minutes of being knocked out of the competition? Then there was that famous Australia–New Zealand match, also in Dublin, when David Campese produced a display that almost took your breath away with its brilliance, its quality and its daring.

The 1995 World Cup was memorable as the event which became synonymous with the new South African nation. For South Africans everywhere, it had the perfect ending. As a Welshman, I couldn't help thinking during that last World Cup, how my own country would be able to support this fine competition. I remember seeing a large banner at the end of that wonderfully tense final in Johannesburg, saying simply: 'See you in Wales '99'. I thought to myself then, 'Yes, and that's not too far away.' The last four years have almost vanished. Although I have been eagerly anticipating the event, nevertheless it has been a time of concern, uncertainty, trepidation, worry, controversy, unease and plenty of other emotions, including hope – hope that we can organise a spectacular World Cup, perhaps the best to date, a tournament that everyone will remember for the rest of their lives. I would like to hear people in fifteen or twenty years' time saying to me, 'Ah, that 1999 World Cup – what a wonderful time we had there, and what fabulous rugby we saw.' That, for me, would be the triumph.

I am proud it is being held in Wales, because of our great tradition in the game. Matches are being played all over Britain, Ireland and France, as happened in 1991, but Wales is where the centre of the event will be. The Welsh Tourist Board have worked very hard to lay the foundations for success for the whole country. Rugby clubs in Wales have been encouraged to adopt an overseas club for the duration of the tournament, and that will surely foster friendships and relationships which may last a lifetime. In other words, one of the great traditions of this game will be carried on.

We have so much to offer in Wales, from spectacular scenery and great food to lovely golf courses. Although it's an old cliché, that famous saying is true – we *will* always have a welcome in the hillsides for everyone, no matter where they are from. As a Welshman, I am proud of that.

I'll tell you a story which epitomises, for me, the kind of welcome and friendship which has played so fundamental a part in the history of this game. In 1983, I was in New Zealand, touring the country not as a player but a follower of the Lions tour, with some rugby people from the British Isles. We were heading for Dunedin to see the Lions' third Test match. We drove from Christchurch and had arranged to stop on the way for some lunch. I had already come to realise how little I had really seen of New Zealand as a player. When you are in the touring squad, you fly from one town to another, exchange one hotel for another and see a different training ground and a different dining room in the hotel restaurant. In 1983, I had the chance to see much more. There were, in all, five coachloads of us on this trip, and we pulled up in a school car park in the town, expecting some pasties and a few beers for a snack lunch. What we got astonished everyone. Laid out before us on long trestle tables was just about every kind of New Zealand delicacy the country had to offer. There were numerous types of fish, lots of different meats, vegetables, salads, pies – it was a real banquet. Almost the whole lot was home-cooked produce.

I talked to the man who had helped lay it on, and tried to

express our genuine thanks for such a wonderful welcome. He just said, 'If what we are giving you here is half as good as you gave us in Wales when I visited your country, I am a happy man.' He had been one of the administrators of a New Zealand touring party that had visited Wales and received excellent hospitality. He and his pals had put on a formidable spread for us, for which so many people had gone to so much trouble. I also talked to some of the women there and asked them about the town and what it was like living there.

'Oh, I'm afraid I have no idea. I live a hundred miles away,' said one. 'We heard that a group of overseas rugby folk were coming through, the people here needed some help and we got involved. We got a few things together, cooked them and brought them here.'

I felt humbled by what they had done for us that day and I will never forget it. For me, it says everything about rugby and explains to some who may not know our sport, just why we feel it is so special.

I hope and believe that the people of Wales will be every bit as welcoming to the many thousands of overseas visitors who will come for the World Cup. I hope we can make it as memorable an experience as that one some friends and I had far away in the south island of New Zealand. If ever that mythical thing called the brotherhood of rugby was apparent, it was on that day.

The next time the World Cup returns to the northern hemisphere, I hope the finals will be held in France. I have enjoyed a long love affair with France and the French way of life and I believe a World Cup staged in France would be a huge success. It is one of the comparatively few rugby-playing countries of the world with an infra-structure suitable for staging the tournament.

Travel is easy. Internal air routes link all the major cities and centres with regular flights, fast motorways snake all over the country and super-fast TGV trains speed passengers through the beautiful French countryside. Paris to Lyons in just two hours? No bother, as my old pal Bill McLaren would say. The food is exquisite, the culture impressive and the weather usually superb, especially down in the south in the autumn. Great towns in the south are steeped in rugby tradition – Beziers, Toulouse, Pau, Perpignan, Toulon, Dax, Biarritz, Narbonne, Grenoble, Brive and Agen – places where rugby union is revered. Besides those obvious venues, there are magnificent stadia at other centres like Nantes, Lens, Saint-Etienne and Bordeaux, grounds capable of holding significant numbers of spectators for the major matches. In Paris, there is the superb Stade de France, a 75,000-seater stadium used for the 1998 football World Cup final.

I can see no reason why France should not hold a rugby World Cup soon. It would be a magnificent experience for everyone visiting the country and their tourist trade would be substantially enhanced by the event. Good luck to them if they campaign for it – they will certainly receive my backing.

CHAPTER NINE

Life After Rugby

The question I am most frequently asked about my playing career and life associated with rugby is 'Do you miss the game?' Well, no I don't, but there are reasons for that.

I knew my playing career was almost over the day I turned down the chance to go on the British Lions tour of New Zealand in 1977. I was married to Maureen with two young kids by then and my priorities were changing. As a young man, I loved the excitement of overseas travel. It was always an adventure. But once I got married, I settled down a little. I'm not suggesting that marriage means carpet slippers and a pipe by the fire for the rest of your life, but anyone who gets married takes on different responsibilities. You want to be with your wife and your family.

I knew that if I went on the Lions tour, I would have to leave my family behind for too long and my business interests would also suffer. I also knew that Wales were due to tour Australia in 1978 where they would play two Tests, and the pressure would be immense on me to make that tour, too. Then, about eighteen months afterwards, the Lions would be back in South Africa for their 1980 tour. I could see this going on forever. I felt that if I didn't make the break, I would be trawling around the world on rugby tours until injuries and failing form reduced me as a player. That worried me no end. You can imagine the sort of conversations there would have been in the pubs and clubs.

'I thought Edwards had a shocker today, didn't you?'

'Aye, he's not the player he was . . .'

That was my worst nightmare and I never wanted it to become reality.

There was much pressure on me to change my mind and go to New Zealand with the Lions, not least from Clive Rowlands who did his best to try to convince me to make the trip. But I knew I'd made the right decision and told him I wouldn't change my mind. I played one more Five Nations Championship season before announcing my retirement, later in 1978.

You don't need to be coaxed to go and play for your country; you shouldn't need to be persuaded to represent the Lions, either. I knew I'd made the right decision about packing up when Wales met the touring New Zealanders at Cardiff in November 1978. I sat in the TV gantry alongside Bill McLaren as the Welsh team ran out, and braced myself to withstand the surge of emotion and regret at not being among them. I sat there, all tensed up waiting for it, but it never came. My heart did not skip a single beat.

So, happy in my mind that I had done the right thing, I could concentrate on other things. I had formed a close association with Jack Hamer, a Neath businessman. It was due to Jack's benevolence that my international career went on until 1978.

The late, great Carwyn James, one of the best coaches I ever worked with (*Colorsport*).

David Duckham scores for James's 1971 Lions in New Zealand. Perhaps we in Wales appreciated his skills more than the English (*Allsport*).

Jeremy Guscott, one of the most exciting players of the modern era. But perhaps another one who England never really got the best out of (*Popperfoto*).

Beating England in Cardiff became a regular event for Wales for over twenty-five years. But we didn't have to deal with Dean Richards then, who was one factor in changing England's luck in 1991 (*Colorsport*).

The hugely physical Gerard Cholley (*left*) of France whose hospitality was awesome in Castres, south of France (*Colorsport*).

Denis Charvet of France had little trouble with defences but a lot more with Neath - or was it my niece? (*Allsport/Billy Stickland*).

Then and Now
Delme Thomas of Llanelli, Wales and the British Lions, (ABOVE) was one of the great line-out operators of his time (*Colorsport*). But lifting (LEFT), which is now permitted, has in many respects reduced the impact of this phase (*Popperfoto*).

tarting a new career as one of the BBC commentary team with Bill McLaren, Nigel armer-Smith and Bill Taylor – the transition wasn't straightforward.

ecognition by St Emilion, during a festival for the first growth. I was able to enjoy me of the local produce afterwards.

Hopes for the Future

A scrum-half I greatly admire: Joost van der Westhuizen of South Africa – his nation's great hope in the 1999 World Cup (*Allsport/Mike Cooper*).

Nelson Mandela, a man for whom I have a deep respect, at Cardiff Castle in June 1998, where he received the freedom of the city (*Popperfoto*).

The magnificent new Millennium Stadium in the heart of Cardiff – its first match saw a famous victory over South Africa (*Allsport/Dave Rogers*).

Graham Henry, the man who has done so much to transform Welsh international rugby and raise hopes for the 1999 World Cup (*Allsport/Dave Rogers*).

With my wife, Maureen, in the garden in 1998.

Playing international rugby and handling its growing commitments without support had become very difficult even by then.
There was already a huge call on a player's time. Lions tours
lasted three and a half months, national tours four to five
weeks. Then there were all the squad sessions prior to the
internationals which meant even more strain on players and any
businesses with which they may have been involved. While I
was still playing, I had nothing but wholehearted support
from Jack, whose company was involved in engineering and
manufacturing.

When I did finally retire, and all the pressures associated with
wondering whether and when to do it evaporated, I recognised
the need to build up a commercial career. Many offers were
made to me, and I took up a few, becoming a non-executive
director on the boards of some companies which were owned
by long-standing friends. In the business world, the twin fields
of sales and marketing were my forte and I continued to work
well with Jack. Several other people wanted me to be a
figurehead but I almost always turned down those approaches. I
didn't want to be paraded as some ex-rugby player; I felt I had
to make my way on my abilities and not rely solely on talents I
may have had in rugby. To succeed in business, you must have
a genuine desire to be involved with a company. I wanted to
contribute, not just be a name on the letterhead. At this time,
although I was getting more and more involved with Jack
Hamer, I still had the flexibility of running my own diary.

As for any activities closely associated with the game, I
believed I could have no more than three or four years 'in the
sun' as it were, before my name was forgotten and someone
else came along. In the meantime, I was determined to make
the most of the opportunities that came my way however long

they might last. It was not only the interesting and worthwhile employment I found in the commercial world which helped make my retirement from the playing side of the game a contented one. The fact that I was soon asked to become a co-commentator for BBC Television, working alongside Bill McLaren, made a huge difference to me. In short, it helped smooth my retirement from the playing side into the media side of the game. I didn't miss rugby because I was still involved as a commentator. Had I finished with the sport one weekend and not been able to retain a firm link with it, it may well not have been as easy to step aside from playing. As it was, I was most fortunate to find myself still going to international matches, still keeping right up to date with the game. I loved doing all that.

The thrill of working alongside Bill McLaren as his co-commentator or analyst was immense. Bill is very knowledgeable about the game, truly an authority on rugby. These days, to have a second commentator working with the main man is considered normal practice, but then the BBC had not really tried it before, not in rugby anyway. It surprised me that, with the notable exception of Cliff Morgan who was head of BBC Outside Broadcasts at the time, no one at the BBC was prepared to give me any real information or training in terms of technique and passing on tips. Here was I, a guy who had been a scrum-half for the last decade, suddenly elevated to the commentary box, and no one seemed to think it worthwhile sitting me down in a studio and going through the basics of the job, such as how to prepare yourself for the work. I was just handed a microphone one afternoon at a match and told to get on with it. Being left to my own devices to that extent astonished me. I was confident enough about my knowledge of the game; it was the technical expertise I lacked. There was also a curious reluctance to set up opportunities for constructive discussion and after-match analysis. I wanted to have some sessions in which we would go through what we had done and work out how we could enhance it. I thought that perhaps I'd get an idea of how to improve my own contributions. But there was nothing beforehand and nothing afterwards. It was just, 'See you at the next match.' I have to admit I found that very disappointing.

I worked for the BBC in that role for eight or nine years from 1978 to season 1985–6. I enjoyed it. I'll always be grateful to the BBC for smoothing my transition from playing career to the next stage of my life.

During those years, I became increasingly aware of the uncertainties of the TV business. It looked a very insecure world from what I could see. Frankly, I wasn't convinced it was for me. Yes, I loved heading off for internationals, keeping in touch with the game, talking to players and working with Bill McLaren. I could see the potential pitfalls, too, and eventually came to the conclusion that I should concentrate my efforts on my commercial interests, but not before I'd had some fun and very amusing experiences – such as when that notorious lady Erica Roe decided to bare all at half-time during an England international at Twickenham. I was with Bill McLaren in the TV gantry and Bill was talking into his microphone, looking down at his monitor as he spoke. I was looking around the ground while listening to what Bill was saying. Suddenly, there was a loud roar and I looked across to see this girl bouncing down the field. Bill, however, completely ignored the fuss as any good professional should, and got on with making his point.

Our producer Bill Taylor was shouting into our ear-pieces,

'Keep going, keep talking – we'll pan in tight and not show it.' It was clear BBC policy not to show streakers. The trouble was, when Bill stopped talking and handed over to me, he looked up, saw Miss Roe and I can still see his expression today. That was my cue; he didn't say another word. The camera shot was on the England team during their half-time talk out on the field but it was the hardest thing in the world not to mention what was going on because the whole team was turning around and looking at the girl. I shouldn't think they took in a word of Bill Beaumont's half-time team-talk. As for me, I had to be perfectly serious while the whole stadium was in uproar, with laughter and jokes all around me. It took all my concentration not to say the wrong thing. Apparently, England scrum-half Steve Smith spotted Erica and said to Bill Beaumont, who had his back to her and was talking away, 'Excuse me Bill, but there's a bird with your backside on her chest coming down the field.'

On another occasion at Twickenham, I left the ground late after doing the commentary with Bill, and was making my way across the dark West car park. Ahead of me, I could see two shadowy figures but the next minute they seemed to disappear, as if into a fence. I had to go that way and soon heard voices coming from behind the fence. From what they were saying, it was clear that nature had made its demands and they had found the nearest safe spot, or so they thought until I replied to something they were saying.

'Oh, I don't agree with that, girls.' There was immediately a loud shriek from behind the fence.

'Oh no, I know that voice,' said one. They couldn't see me and I couldn't see them, but we were close enough to hear one another speak.

'You won't tell anyone, will you,' said one of the voices.

'Of course not, girls,' I said, hurrying off to my car. The things you see and hear at rugby grounds on big match days!

It's probably true to say that everyone associated with TV gets a buzz of adrenalin on the big day. Whether it's the producer, commentator, cameraman or anyone else, the sense of occasion is immense for everyone. When things go wrong, as they can do, nerves can get pretty frayed.

I was in Ireland for one international and we were down on the side of the pitch, waiting to do a pre-match interview. I don't think there has ever been a time when I've been to Ireland and everything has worked out as it should, so perhaps I was half expecting trouble. You would be in the commentary box and someone would say, 'The microphones are down,' meaning a technical fault had occurred somewhere in the system and, although our lips moved, no sound was heard. Sometimes, we would have to use the radio link or speak down the telephone lines. While you were talking, trying to sound calm and composed, some engineers from the Irish TV station, RTE, would be hanging precariously from the sheer cliff face that was the front of the grandstand facing you, desperately searching for the loose connection which had sabotaged the microphones.

I remember on one particular day we were about to do a live link-up with David Coleman back in the *Grandstand* studio in London, when someone suddenly shouted into our ear-pieces, 'We've lost all pictures to London.' There wasn't immediate panic; after all, this wasn't unknown and they usually turned up. But with two minutes to go, and London saying they still couldn't get a picture out of Dublin, people were starting to get a bit edgy, not to say panicky. Bill Taylor, our producer, was doing his nut by this time and shouting at his cameramen to help.

One burly local camera operator decided to try a particularly subtle method of getting the pictures back. With ninety seconds left before transmission was due to start live from London, the Irishman picked up a hefty block of wood and simply whacked the top of the camera. Had a stranger done it, he'd have been arrested and charged with criminal damage. Lo and behold, the screens at Lansdowne Road suddenly flickered into life and there came an excited shout down the line from London: 'We've got pictures, pictures back.' The wonders of modern technology!

Another reason I was glad to be involved with the BBC once I'd finished playing rugby, was that it demanded a discipline I was pleased to follow. As a player, you were of course always careful about what you ate and drank before games. Once you step down from that level, the need for that discipline can disappear. But because I was working for TV, I knew I had to maintain it. When I was working, I always tried to get a decent night's sleep before a big game and I'd rarely touch a drink before commentary.

I took it seriously and started to have weird dreams. I'd suddenly start to panic, believing I couldn't get into a ground for some reason such as losing my ticket. I'd dream that I was really late, I could hear Bill McLaren starting his commentary and I couldn't find the right entrance to reach the TV commentary box. I would be going round and round some stadium desperate to get in, and it was getting later and later. Perhaps the match would have already started and I'd be in a real panic until I woke up with a start.

In fact, it almost happened to me at Murrayfield in 1999,

where I was due to commentate on the Scotland–Wales Five Nations Championship match. A taxi dropped me where I thought I had to go to join up with my colleagues at BBC Wales. But Murrayfield is so big these days that I couldn't get my bearings and didn't know where I was supposed to be. I asked three gatemen and they weren't sure either, and time was starting to tick by. There I was, limping around the outside of this vast stadium, my arthritic knees starting to cause me trouble, and wondering where on earth I should go. Fortunately, I did find the way eventually and arrived in time.

In the early 1980s, I was caught up in a very disagreeable affair involving the newspaper to which I was contributing a column at that time, the *News of the World*. Rugby was changing significantly by then and you could see the difficulties coming. A man named Arthur Young befriended us over a period of time when I was still representing Wales. Arthur, who worked for Adidas, the sports goods manufacturer that was becoming extremely successful, approached us before one Welsh international and explained his position. He wanted to offer us some of the company's sports and leisure wear, free of charge of course, but in return he wanted prominent publicity for his company. What he proposed was that we wear a pair of Adidas boots, instantly recognisable by the three white stripes which ran down the side of the boot. We tried out the boots and, had we been rugby players in the south of France where you just wanted a soft shoe in which you could run on the top of the ground, we would probably have found them ideal. But they were too soft for the yielding, muddy grounds of Wales and besides, you wouldn't want to wear new boots for the first time at an international. So Arthur took away our regular boots, fabulous things made by the G.T. Law specialist company, and painted three white stripes down them. We knew and liked Arthur by this time. So we let him do it. No money was involved. We were totally naive and never appreciated the implications until it was too late.

Nothing was mentioned about it again. But as time went on, other manufacturers started to come to us and ask us if we would like to wear their gear, too. Then, we were given some money to do so. It wasn't much even by the standards of those days, let alone today. The biggest reward was that we could have any amount of kit we wanted over a period of time. As for the money, we were led to believe that the tax had been paid at source. As I say, we were new to this sort of thing and naive.

Nothing much happened about it until a few years after I retired. Then Arthur Young, in his words, wanted to show up the hypocrisy of the Welsh Rugby Union, blew the gaff and told the *News of the World* about how he'd paid Welsh players to wear Adidas gear. It was a betrayal of the company by a former employee but it caused a furore in rugby circles.

By the time the story emerged, I was writing for the *News of the World* and, having been mentioned by Arthur who'd said I was involved, the paper called me and said they wanted me to name other names. I flatly refused. My loyalty to my former playing colleagues was too strong for that. The paper didn't say a lot when I told them I wouldn't do it, but they did not renew my contract when it ended soon after, and I always felt that was the reason. I had been with the paper for four or five years and at best it seemed highly coincidental. I have never regretted not shopping my old playing pals.

Since then I have never been involved with another newspaper on an exclusive basis. I have concentrated on TV and radio for BBC Wales. I have enjoyed the freedom that has given me, because it didn't commit me every single weekend. I would do the internationals, of course, and sometimes go to Bridgend or Swansea for a match. I still kept my involvement without feeling it was dominating my life.

During this time, I was also appearing on several TV shows, including the BBC's *Question of Sport* with Emlyn Hughes. That ran for two or three series from the start of the 1980s and from it came opportunities for one-off appearances, such as speaking at functions, opening new buildings and attending dinners as guest speaker. I was kept very busy.

One invitation was to be part of the judging panel for a combined 'Miss Wales' and 'Miss England' beauty contest held in Morocco with international TV coverage. It was a fabulous location and I was there for three or four days. Well, as I told Maureen later, someone had to make those sacrifices to ensure all the girls had a fair judging!

My association with the event may have been somewhat tenuous but the journey over there was to have profound consequences for me and my future business career. On the train journey from Wales up to London, *en route* to Heathrow airport, I met John Elfed Jones, who had just taken the position of Chairman of the new Welsh Water Authority. John saw me on the train and said, 'Ah, Gareth, you are just the man I want to see.' It turned out that he had been asked by the Secretary of State for Wales, Nicholas Edwards (now Lord Crickhowell), to set up a small board to run the authority. A statutory position on the board would go to the Chairman of the Regional Fisheries Advisory Committee. That person would advise the authority on all fishing matters. John was well aware of my fishing interests and from that chance meeting, I was to become involved. After privatisation they became Welsh Water plc and I am still with them. Also at John's invitation, I subsequently joined the board as Chairman of Welsh Water plc's subsidiary, 'Hamdden' which is the Welsh word for leisure. My responsibilities covered such concerns as several up-market country houses, hotels, and salmon fishing interests and beats on the River Tywi. In addition, there was the management of all the aquatic sports on our reservoirs throughout Wales to think about.

I had always been passionately interested in many of these matters through my love of fishing, but I think it's fair to say I was unaware of the political minefield that was the Welsh Fisheries industry. During the course of the next six to seven years, I found myself being forced to juggle the interests of many interested parties – the netsmen, the coarse fishermen, the game fishermen, the rod and line anglers, the commercial netsmen, the owners, the angling club officials. I had to chair regular meetings between representatives of all these interests and try to accommodate the wishes of all the diverse parties, none of whom ever saw eye to eye. Twice a year, we would meet the Minister of Agriculture, Fisheries and Food for discussions.

Before becoming chairman of Hamdden, I had been a fisherman with a keen interest in just catching fish. I hadn't realised there were far wider issues such as a genuine concern for the decline of the salmon stock throughout Wales. I greatly welcomed the opportunity to have a genuine input into policies that would affect the future of the fishing industry.

I was somewhat apprehensive about taking up the post in the first place. The previous Chairman, who had had to retire, was the formidable Admiral Sir Thomas Pearson, a former head of NATO. As I later found out, in one sense I was right to have reservations. The role was supposed to take up one day a week, no more except on very special occasions. But once I began to get involved, I quickly came to realise that I needed to give the job much more time than that. Hardly a day went by without someone coming up to me wanting to discuss some aspect of the work. They were by no means complimentary much of the time, either! It wasn't a job to be in if I was searching for plaudits. Luckily, I wasn't put out if someone came up to me and said, 'You're trying to throw the netsmen off the rivers,' or, 'You're just not giving the coarse fishermen enough consideration.'

I remember one day I had to attend an England–Wales rugby match at Twickenham as part of my work in the world of corporate business entertainment. I'd driven up with some friends in a specially hired car and got there early because I was also working for BBC's *Grandstand*. Afterwards, I returned to the North car park exhausted, and sat down in the back of the car for a few minutes to have a short rest. Suddenly, I was aware of a commotion outside the car. There stood a well-built woman with a flushed complexion, looking pretty upset and angry about something. Some of my friends and colleagues were trying to restrain her. Immediately she saw me, she launched into a volley of criticism over my role as Chairman of Hamdden.

'You, it's all your fault,' she said to me. 'You are trying to throw the netsmen off the rivers.' In the middle of the Twickenham car park, someone was really worked up about matters concerning the waterways back in Wales. There was I thinking she'd wanted to berate the Welsh rugby selectors for their latest team, and was seeking my support!

These difficulties were small by comparison with the overall task. I genuinely loved the job and it has given me a wonderful insight into the business. Fishing has been a major part of my life from my earliest days when I stood above the river in the village where we lived, clutching a long bamboo pole with a bent pin on one end with a piece of twine attached to it.

Poaching presented us with a huge problem. There is a widespread misconception that the term 'poaching' means simply a village man taking one fish for the pot. Whether there is anything essentially wrong with that isn't for me to say, although I don't condone it. Such people are still breaking the law, but it isn't them the authorities really have in mind. What caused the greatest concern to us then and still does in the world of fisheries and water is the mass poaching of salmon in the estuaries with very sophisticated machinery such as extremely light micro-nets that are miles long. These fine mesh nets have sonar and are used to ensnare hundreds and thousands of salmon illegally. In recent years, they have been responsible for decimating the salmon stocks. What concerned me equally was the rather dismissive attitude of certain officials at the Ministry of Agriculture and Fisheries when we came to discuss these matters. That used to upset me almost as much as the fact that stocks of this wonderful fish were being seriously reduced all the while.

This problem remains as serious today as it was a few years ago, perhaps more so. You only have to look at the Wye, a river that was once renowned for salmon, to see the effect. The Wye used to be one of the major rivers in England and Wales for salmon. Alas, the salmon runs are decreasing dramatically. It has seen a rapid decline in numbers even with voluntary measures of preservation in place on the river.

Greater access to the rivers means more fishing and the exploitation of obvious commercial possibilities. The pressure on the salmon has increased to such an extent that there is a long-term threat to the future of this lovely fish. Will future generations have the opportunity to fish for salmon with rod and line? That has always been my concern and it remains more of a worry today than ever before. Fishing for salmon and sea trout has brought me a tremendous amount of pleasure over the years. I have fished some of the finest rivers in Europe but as every year has passed, I have seen some of these magnificent rivers suffering from a growing lack of stock. That has to be a concern for everybody.

Surely the government could make some brave decisions about the illegal catching of salmon on the high seas and help reintroduce juvenile stocks of the fish into our rivers. The world of the salmon is fascinating. They start their life high up in the mountain streams and make their way to sea for one or two years to mature. After that, it is part of nature's recycling programme that they come back into the rivers to re-generate. But with modern technology used at sea, whole stocks can be intercepted and caught before they can return to the rivers. Decimating these stocks is threatening the whole future of this fish.

Salmon poaching continues in plenty of other forms, such as by the unscrupulous gangs who net rivers. But the biggest concern by far has to be this unlawful netting on the high seas. Policing such illegal activities is very difficult and costly, but as someone who has known the passion and love of this sport and the great fish for so many years, I believe that no price is too high to pay to maintain this magnificent species.

When the water authority was privatised, the choice for me was either to go to the National Rivers Authority under the environmental agencies or to follow John Elfed Jones into the newly organised private sector and the leisure side of the business. I did the latter and am still enjoying my role in the business. Today, I help with the promotion of the plc at various functions.

I also have business associations with Stan and Peter Thomas. Peter is the Chairman of Cardiff Rugby Club and Stan, Chairman of TBI plc, which is one of the biggest airport operators in the world, owning among others Cardiff and Belfast airports. TBI is one of Wales's great success stories in the business world. Seeing Stan today, a major business player in Welsh life, makes me realise how far he has come from the lad I first met when I was eighteen in the Cardiff Rugby Club dressing-room. Stan was wearing the No. 9 shirt, ready to play in a trial for Cardiff, until Keith Rowlands, then Cardiff's captain, introduced me to him with the immortal words, 'Stan, would you give Gareth your shirt? You're playing in Saturday's trial, not today's.' Well, Stan never got to play in that shirt again but we still struck up a friendship which has lasted thirty years. When I won my fiftieth cap, I gave my jersey to Stan, joking, 'I took one shirt off your back all those years ago – now I'm giving you one back.' He has it framed at his home, a famous jersey on the wall in Jersey.

When I won that fiftieth cap, I became the first player to reach a half century of games for Wales and the WRU kindly decided to award me a special cap to commemorate the achievement. Normally, you receive only one cap no matter how many times you represent Wales. Now I had a second.

Some time later, I was approached by NASA in America. The father of one of the astronauts about to go into space was from Cardiff and he had brought up his son on stories of rugby. His son had been born in Wales and regarded himself very much as a Welshman, the first who would go into space. I was asked if I had anything that I could loan them, a small artefact they could carry into space. One of my most prized possessions has always been that fiftieth cap so I sent it to them and off they went. Watching the news and seeing these guys spinning round inside their tiny capsule up in space with one of them wearing my fiftieth cap was an extraordinary experience. The cap, like the crew, came back safely and I have it together with a plaque from NASA which says the cap went six and a half million miles around earth, or some such distance. I am most proud of it.

Besides all this, I still have my work for BBC Wales and S4C, the Welsh language channel for whom I help provide match coverage most weekends. I attend games all over Wales and also at the Five Nations international grounds when that great Championship begins early in the New Year, which I enjoy immensely.

My involvement as a non-executive director of Cardiff Rugby Club also keeps me close to rugby. Cardiff is the only senior club I ever played for, and I am delighted to be able to put something back into a club that gave me so much pleasure throughout my playing career. I see part of my role as trying to help guide them through some pretty stormy waters that the impact of professionalism has brought to the sport. I have been saddened to see the hostility and obstructionist attitude of the Welsh Rugby Union to so much of what clubs like Cardiff have tried to do. Instead of finding support from an authority to whom we could turn for help, advice and encouragement, Cardiff – together with Swansea – were forced to leave the WRU fraternity. That was sad for both clubs and Union, and I believe for the game at large.

We had no choice. The Union's demand that we sign

ten-year loyalty agreements was totally unrealistic in the profes-sional era. Which company ties itself to another for ten years in the modern-day business climate? Events move so swiftly these days that five years would be an eternity. I hoped the WRU would understand this, but instead they tried to hound us back into the fold.

The point was, had we stayed within the Welsh League we would have been bankrupt within twelve months. The crowds were no longer interested in supporting us in sufficient num-bers when we hosted matches against clubs like Newport, Ebbw Vale, Neath, Caerphilly and Aberavon. That is not meant to be disrespectful to those clubs or any of the others in Wales. But what people wanted was to see us resume our traditional fixtures against the powerful English club sides – Bath, Gloucester, Leicester, Wasps and Harlequins. When we finally took the only road open to us and went off to arrange Anglo–Welsh matches against those clubs for season 1998–9, the people of Wales voted with their feet. Our attendances and receipts went through the roof and it became common for us to have anything between 8,000 and 12,000 plus for one of those games.

We were barred from the Welsh League competition, and eventually fined £150,000. But I am pleased to say harmony and agreement have at last been reached.

Whichever club you support, no one in Wales can pretend that clubs of the stature of Cardiff and Swansea do not matter. They are entitled to a voice, and to run their own affairs in a proper business-like manner. Ideally, that would be within the WRU, but the Union simply attempted to veto all ideas coming from the clubs and put obstacles in our path. So we had to forge ahead in our own direction. We regretted having to do it but given the attitude of so many people on the WRU, we had little choice but to make our own way in a world which required sufficient numbers of supporters to come through our gates in order to fund our commitments under professionalism. Rugby is now a business, not just a sport. Balance sheets have to make economic sense and if one approach is not working, another must be found.

One of the initiatives Cardiff have been working hard on is something called 'Capital Rugby', of which I am in charge. What we have set out to do is create official links between the club and various schools in the area, with the aim of fostering interest in rugby and getting more youngsters to play the game. I have mentioned earlier that a disturbing number of youngsters are no longer playing rugby in Wales. At Cardiff, we felt we should try to do something about it. Creating more interest in the game among schoolchildren is the first step, but we realised it would be difficult. In fact, I wondered how much interest there would be in such a scheme and half expected just a handful of people to drift along for the official launch.

The reality took not only me by surprise but everyone associated with the scheme. The place was packed with people; the interest was phenomenal. You could see the importance of it by those who attended – rugby officials such as Graham Henry, the Wales coach, several members of the WRU and the Chairman of the local council.

It is a partnership arrangement between Cardiff Rugby Club, the schools wishing to take part, local businesses and council authorities. Its aim is simple; to bring the game back into the schools. We lost our base for rugby when the schools system was changed twenty or so years ago. So we have tried to co-ordinate all the schools in the Cardiff area to make sure nobody slips through the net but also to reintroduce the general benefits of playing the game. Rugby is a game which can be lots of fun for boys and girls. We want to show them that, to entice young children and families, too, to come and support the game in greater numbers. We think it will help the local clubs. The reason we went through the local schools was that we wanted to avoid a club against club conflict. We felt it was less political this way. The kids can do as they wish. They can play for whichever club they want eventually. All we are trying to do is remind them that rugby is here for them and give them the opportunity to try it.

The days are long gone when we in Wales could afford to sit back and the production line would just keep churning out thousands upon thousands of young rugby players. I am pleased that my generation is not repeating the mistake made by those who were in charge of the sport twenty years ago who sat back and did next to nothing, assuming rugby would always be king in Wales. That error must never be repeated.

There has been a deep empathy between Wales and the sport of rugby union, perhaps more so than any other game. Our culture, our roots, our national identity have all been closely entwined with this sport. To expect that always to be the case, to assume nothing would change it and therefore a minimum of effort was required to stimulate the next generation, was an awful mistake. The generation I played with and against, has come to recognise that error and does not intend to let it occur again.

What has pleased me most about Cardiff's idea is that everyone has been so supportive. To see youngsters coming and playing rugby, no matter what standard they are, and to hear words of encouragement for what we are trying to do from schoolteachers and parents, have made it very worthwhile. I am optimistic that the scheme will continue to flourish, to grow in size and become an important part of these youngsters' lives.

Sport offers valuable opportunities for young people – fitness, recreation, enjoyment and, if required, a competitive edge. All of these are highly beneficial to the young.

Overall, my interests are as diverse as my lifestyle. I play golf and go fishing, both of which activities I still adore. I've been casting the fly for more years than I care to remember but the pleasure of doing so, of standing in water perhaps somewhere in the beautiful Scottish borders or in a river deep in the lovely Welsh countryside, remains one of the delights of my life.

I didn't take up golf seriously until 1983 but long ago realised how much it has given me, and how it has broadened my life. There's nothing better than getting out on the course with some friends and having a wonderful day.

Rugby was a great part of my life, and I loved every minute of my playing days, but I knew that once I had finished, I'd played the game out of my system. That fact probably explains why I have never felt a sense of loss during my retirement. I did what I wanted to do in it – and more – and I was very fortunate to be able to do that. But all good things must end and I have never lamented that fact. The world is too full of enticing opportunities to look back and regret anything much. I am glad to say I have never done that in my life.

CHAPTER TEN

Injuries

I can think of a very large group of my former playing colleagues at both club and international level, who would laugh themselves senseless at the idea of my discussing injuries.

'Never had any, what does he know about them?' they might say. To be fair, they'd have a point. Strained and sore hamstrings I could tell you a bit about; I had a good few of those in my playing career. But apart from those and the usual bumps and bruises, I have to admit I was extremely lucky to survive thirteen years in senior rugby without a single major injury. I never had one stitch put into my body to sew up torn skin. I never broke a bone, never suffered any kind of injury requiring a long lay-off from the sport. I find it puzzling.

I'm sure I didn't hang back. I frequently seemed to get collared by large forwards, which is part and parcel of a scrum-half's trade. The player who doesn't fancy some big hits from tough old forwards shouldn't go anywhere near the No. 9 shirt. You are right in there beside the forwards, the link between your pack and backs. Getting the ball away as quickly and cleanly as possible is a big part of your game. Spotting opportunities to do the unexpected is also fundamental to the job. When you see any good scrum-half play, he should be constantly on the look-out for chances to break through the opposition's defences. That might be down the blindside at a ruck or maul, even a set scrum, or it could be round either the front or back of the line-out. It could mean burrowing straight through the forwards in front of you. Actually taking the ball back into your pack is sometimes necessary if it is poor quality possession. Better that than shipping it out to your stand-off half, and seeing him buried by a couple of back row hunters from the opposing team.

So taking plenty of knocks is to be expected if you call yourself a scrum-half. Yet the fact remains that I was virtually injury free when I retired from top-class rugby. I felt that as I had walked away from the game in that condition, I'd be the fortunate one, the guy who would disprove all those tales from gnarled rugby men of yesteryear that if you play this game, you pay a price in later years. Well not me, bach, I thought to myself. But as I reach my fifties, I realise that I am no different from most other ex-rugby players. Middle age is presenting me with a bill to pay for those great years when I played the game and so enjoyed it.

It's important to put this whole subject in the right context. If you were to ask me whether I now regret playing rugby for so many years, especially at the top level where the tackles and knocks were inevitably harder, I would think you daft. Of course I don't, how could I? Regret all those fantastic memories? Regret the thrill of so many major occasions, some wonderful victories and the winning of Test series and Grand

Slams? Regret having met all those wonderful people around the world? Regret having seen so many countries of the world and visited places I could never have imagined seeing but for my sport? Never. All I am saying is that whatever state you are in when you leave the game, you will find that it does catch up with you in later life. It is part of the deal, as the Americans like to say.

There are days when I limp around my home, or the golf course, resembling some old man from the local allotment society. Believe me, it is not done for effect, but because of the severe pain I feel in both knees – the same knees that never had cartilage trouble or, worse still, medial or cruciate ligament damage. There is not very much that can be done about it at the moment, but a knee replacement operation may be for me in the future.

None of this will come as much of a surprise to many of my playing contemporaries, such as Jean Pierre Rives who once played a rugby international against Australia in Sydney fourteen days after dislocating his shoulder four times in a game against New South Wales. Rives was pumped full of painkillers, strapped up until he resembled the Hunchback of Notre Dame and then, with one arm hanging uselessly down his side, proceeded to go out and make tackles beside hanging on to the side of the scrum. Ever since, Jean Pierre has paid the price for such an extraordinary act of courage.

Perhaps Jean Pierre was a special case; he had his own particular brand of bravery. But plenty of other rugby players I knew in my era played when they weren't a hundred per cent fit, and acknowledged the likely consequences. They got on with it and grumbled to no one.

When you played an international against a country like

France, you knew full well what you were letting yourself in for. It would be a gruelling examination of your mental and physical capacity, sometimes with outright violence involved when things got out of hand. They put hard men into the world of international rugby union; those players brought a certain reputation to the arena and were usually determined to live down to it. Even those Frenchmen who did not step across the line of tolerance into a murkier world of premeditated violence, still played the game with a frightening intensity and commitment. It was only what we expected.

Now, sitting in the safety and comfort of the stand at a rugby international, I wonder about the current generation playing the game. If we thought the game was hard enough when we played it, today's version is something else. I don't accept that the modern-day player is necessarily any harder or tougher. We had some real hard men around in our day. What about Charlie Faulkner, Bobby Windsor and Graham Price, for starters; Geoff Wheel, the Swansea second row forward, was no soft touch, either. There were plenty more like them.

Colin Meads of New Zealand springs to mind. He worked long hours each day on his farm and the physical work built him up into a tremendously strong man. Meads was regarded as the toughest man in the world game at one stage in the late 1960s. Equate that with some of the players who have played the game in more recent years, or those who are currently doing so. The Australian captain John Eales stands 6 feet 6½ inches and weighs 18 stone 3lbs. The South African lock Krynauw Otto is the same size. England lock Wade Dooley was 6 feet 8 inches, 17 stone 9lbs. Given that Meads was regarded in his day as absolutely fearsome, an enormous man, these statistics demonstrate one difference in the game since the Te Kuiti sheep farmer played it. Players are physically bigger, and the hits made in tackles are certainly more explosive. Some of them make even me shudder, and I took the tackles of some of the most powerful South Africans and New Zealanders.

I cannot help but be concerned for the future of the modern-day rugby player. One of the key issues here is the way the game is now played. It was tough enough in my era; they did things like stand on your head. It is probably cleaner now because of the greater attention given to foul play; the contribution of the two touch judges at matches is an important element in this. Suddenly, the player committing foul play has to avoid six eyes, not just two, and that increases his chances of getting caught and punished. But the play is totally different. Today, the accent seems to be on bashing into each other. A lot of the subtlety has gone – instead of trying to find open space, players seek the tackler to take him out and set up the next phase of play. This involves head-on collisions at high speed, explosive impact blows which must have an effect on the body. These type of collisions have become commonplace.

When a forward of, say, 16 stone or more charges at a back with his knees pumping, it is quite a sight. The defending three-quarter has to make sure his tackling technique is spot-on because otherwise not only is he in danger of missing the tackle but also of getting injured. But when a forward of, say, 18 stone or more gets up a head of steam and, at full pace, crashes into a defending forward who is of similar proportions, you have a collision which at pace produces a very considerable impact. A 36-stone collision between two big forwards is body against body, bone against bone. I don't believe the human body was designed for such impacts.

Another aspect of the modern game which concerns me is the tendency to patch up injuries and play through them. Although, as I've mentioned, in my day plenty of players went on when not fully fit, now it seems to be done as a matter of course and with more serious injuries. It is probably a manifestation of professionalism. Highly paid players are inevitably under more pressure to play than an amateur doing it for his love of the sport. The latter could not be so easily coerced into playing on through an injury because financial reward was not involved. But when a player is earning £100,000 or £150,000 a year, as some are, he is in a very different situation. The extra demands of the professional game then emerge.

My philosophy concerning injuries was simple. If I thought it would take a week to regain fitness, invariably it took two. Trying to rush back and make it in one week usually had repercussions and you'd eventually find yourself spending even more time on the sidelines. But now, club owners do not want expensively recruited players sitting in the grandstand very often. The pressures are there to hurry injuries, to make do and go out and play when less than fully fit. Some players have injections put into soft tissue injuries, which are supposed to aid the healing process, to speed it up. In my career, I never missed a game for Wales through injury but I never took injections to play in a match. I don't know what the long-term cost of doing so is, and that worries me about modern-day rugby players.

I took my own health for granted. I suffered no serious injuries, yet a few years ago, I woke up one morning with creaking knees which have now deteriorated to the extent that they restrict my activities. I think to myself, 'If this has happened to me, then God help those guys who are playing today, taking the big hits and playing when they really aren't quite ready after an injury.' The long-term cost for them may prove enormous.

For them, sadly, there is no way around the problem. You can only play the game the way it has evolved. They have to cope and they do, in terms of superior physical preparation and after-match care. Our after-match programme meant a good few beers at the club, then off out for a great night. The next day would be spent trying to get over the combination of the match and the night out before getting ready to go back to work on Monday morning. Today, players are into the after-match programme the minute the final whistle blows. They're often seen winding down by jogging gently around the emptying ground, before getting showered and changed. The next morning after a quiet night at home, they are in the swimming pool easing away the aches and strains.

The modern-day player is much more protected than in our day. Forwards wear neck and shoulder padding which cushions some of the impacts. But if they believe it will save them from the long-term problems, they are probably kidding themselves. It is the explosive impact of collisions, the blows on joints and all the twists and turns which do the damage to the body.

When I started having trouble with my knees, I saw a couple of doctors. They came out with virtually the same reaction – 'What do you expect?' There was a slight air of astonishment in their voices. Both said they would have anticipated nothing else but such problems at that stage of my life after years of playing a physically demanding sport at the top level. One of them told me, 'Let's be honest. You have abused your body. It was not designed for all that.' He meant it in the nicest way, and of course he was right. The wear and tear from thousands of kicks, hard tackles, major collisions, bumps and bruises all have a jarring effect on the human body, which isn't designed to withstand such treatment. I keep returning to that haunting thought – how will today's players be in twenty-five years time?

The physical dangers of rugby football are always a concern, and must continue to be so especially with some of the bad injuries of recent years such as that suffered by Gwyn Jones. He was captain of Wales when he was temporarily paralysed in a collision while playing for Cardiff. An injury like that brings it home to you. There's no getting away from the basic point – rugby, statistically, is a dangerous game.

I have a brother-in-law who is an orthopaedic surgeon and have discussed this subject with him many times. Also, as a parent, when I watch children playing rugby, I always harbour some slight concern in the back of my mind about injuries. I'm not saying that parents standing on a school field touchline should be frozen with fear that their child might be paralysed at any minute. That would be silly. There are risks involved in most activities and you can't cocoon children, stopping them having fun. It would not be right to prevent children climbing trees because they might fall down, or riding a bike because a car might knock them over. Life is full of risks and you have to keep all such things in perspective. When I played rugby, I don't suppose I once thought about the dangers of playing but of course when you become a parent and your child starts to get involved, it comes into your mind.

What is important in rugby is that children are taught to tackle correctly at an early age. The technique required can be easily learned and it is vital this is done. Get the technique wrong and you could find yourself in real trouble. A lot of injuries come from lack of knowledge and technique. Nowadays a career in rugby can be very lucrative, so it becomes even more essential that kids learn at an early stage the fundamentals of the sport's technique. Once they master that, they are at least properly equipped to handle most things apart from the freak accident, against which there can never be total insurance.

For me, rugby remains a game without peer. When it is played well, there isn't anything to rival it – the exhilaration of passing a ball at speed, of racing clear to score a try, of making a hard tackle and of being involved.

Our sons, Owen and Rhys, both play the game and not because I demanded they do so – I made up my mind long ago that I would be the last father to push them into the sport I had played. I feel it would have been the worst thing I could have done to overburden the lads with the game at a young age, to ram rugby down their throats from the moment they could pick up a ball. Had either or both of our sons never wanted to go near a rugby ball in their entire lives, I wouldn't have had the slightest problem with that, although I can't deny I was happy when they did play because they wanted to.

It seems to me that youngsters often play soccer to start off because it is so much easier to play. Not only is it fun, but it also helps them to acquire the basic skills that will serve them well if they then go on to play rugby. This is just about what happened in our household. The boys eventually decided they wanted to play rugby. More often than not, I would stand aside from conversations on the subject. Today, I admit, I wonder whether I stood away too much. In the event, they played for their local school before moving on to Millfield where they emulated their father by playing for the first XV. By a pleasant twist of fate, Rhys was a member of Millfield's winning VII at the Rosslyn Park Public Schools Sevens tournament at Roe-hampton, exactly thirty years after I had played in the same event and been a part of Millfield's successful side.

Owen played for Cardiff Youth for a while and later made his debut for the first XV. He also enjoyed rugby at university but then went abroad for some time. Now, he is in a job which curtails serious rugby. Rhys followed his brother into the Cardiff Youth side then played a very competitive season with the Tondu club, in the Welsh second division. They still play social rugby and Owen travels regularly to London to play for Millfield Old Boys.

I am proud of both our sons for the way they have handled what I suppose some would describe as an air of expectation in rugby at the family name. It's ridiculous to make comparisons; both the boys' lives have taken a different course from mine. It can be hard for the children of successful sportsmen or politi-cians following in their parents' footsteps. How much was Liam Botham's choice of rugby over cricket guided by the fact that he would always have been compared to his father, Ian? The world never seems to run out of insensitive people who say the wrong thing at the wrong time. I'm pleased to say that I think our sons have coped with it extremely well over the years. It hasn't bothered them at all as far as I can see. Their dad is just their dad to them, and that's certainly how I would want it to be.

CHAPTER ELEVEN

The Pleasure Principle

I t seemed a reasonable decision to make at the time, but
looking back now, a few years later, I don't believe I have
ever regretted the ordering of a simple meal quite as
much.

Maureen and I had found ourselves delayed at Heathrow
Airport early one evening in 1987, awaiting a flight to Toulouse
in the south of France. The reason for our trip was that I had
broken my avowed promise never to play any more rugby. My
rather lame excuse was that it was a special occasion, a one-off.
I had been asked to appear in a celebration match which was to
take place in Castres, the rugby town some seventy-five kilo-
metres east of Toulouse. It was the 'Jubilee de Cholley'. Local
hero Gerard Cholley had played in the 1977 French Grand
Slam-winning side, and this was the tenth anniversary.

Gerard is one of the great men of French rugby. In his
playing days, he was an absolute bear of a man who stood 6 feet
3 inches and weighed 16 stone 7lbs. As a prop forward, he was
probably too big to be a technical genius in his trade but his

sheer brute strength made him an opponent widely feared and respected. Gerard was a boxer at one time in his earlier sporting life and with hands the size of his, it wasn't hard to believe. If anyone ever upset Monsieur Cholley on a rugby field, they risked a right hook that could demolish even some of the most proficient in the pugilists' business.

I had played very few physical contact games since my retirement in 1978. I figured that it would be only too likely that, having got through my playing career without a major injury, I'd turn out in some charity match and break a leg or something. Life tends to be that way, doesn't it? In 1978, I did play for an invitation soccer team. It was a match at Anfield for the testimonial of Chris Lawler, that fine Liverpool full-back. But as for rugby, I'd studiously avoided all the requests, urgings and pleadings to put on my boots again, until Monsieur Cholley came calling. In his broken English, with a voice as gentle as his frame was massively intimidating, Gerard said, 'Gareth, please come.' I didn't want to let down an old opponent whom I had come to respect a very great deal.

Trouble was, Gerard's invitation match turned out to be scheduled for the weekend of that violent storm which raged across southern England, the worst for three hundred years. Seve Ballesteros was playing in a golf tournament at Wentworth at the time and I remember reading that he'd got up the morning after, seen the utter devastation of trees brought down all around the home he had rented somewhere on the Wentworth estate and said, 'It was how I imagined Vietnam, it seemed as if the world had ended.'

Just getting from Wales to Heathrow Airport was difficult enough. Of course, the plane was delayed which meant we all had a problem. We'd been invited to a dinner once we reached

Castres but we realised that we weren't likely to arrive until two or three the next morning. Several of us had gathered at Heathrow to make the trip, including Fergus Slattery and Ken Kennedy. By common consent, we decided it would be a good idea to have a meal while we could, because there would be scant likelihood of eating by the time we did arrive. So off we trooped to one of the airport restaurants. I think we had steak and chips washed down with a few bottles of red wine. I enjoy such occasions; it is the chance to have a good chat with old friends and playing colleagues and their wives. It is informal and extremely pleasant.

After a while, we felt we'd eaten and drunk more than enough and, soon after, our flight was called. On board, the captain was conciliatory. 'Air France apologises for the delay to our flight tonight. This is due to the bad weather. We hope you will have a comfortable flight to Toulouse.'

It quickly became apparent it would be comfortable. No sooner had we taken off than champagne and smoked salmon were served to our group, and you got the impression that they weren't counting the number of bottles offered! By the time the plane arrived in Toulouse and we had been greeted by Gerard with one of his bone-crushing handshakes, we were not ready for much else. The trouble was, a lot else was planned.

After a drive at breakneck speed to Castres, Gerard said we might as well just look in at the clubhouse where the dinner had been planned for that night. But of course, as it was now well past one o'clock in the morning, that was long since over, or so we thought. We were greeted by a throng of supporters, and given more champagne. Almost at once, huge silver trays piled with lobster and supported by bottles of white burgundy were carried into the room to the accompaniment of great applause.

Suddenly, the evening had come alive again.

But alas, this was the mere preliminary course! Having consumed the wondrous seafood and white wine, our plates were cleared and replaced, very quickly, by the high point of the feast – trays full of chateaubriand with copious bottles of exceptional red burgundy. We made a worthy stab at this, and when we had done our best, the cheese course arrived. Anyone who has ever eaten a serious meal in the south of France doesn't need me to tell them what that course entails. With every course, a different wine was produced. This gastronomic *tour de force* finally approached its conclusion in the old sports clubhouse as the clock ticked close to 4 a.m., with a large bottle of vintage brandy which was put on the table – *pour le digéstif*.

I wouldn't say that our bed sagged dangerously as we climbed into it sometime around four thirty that morning, but let's suggest that we all ought to be grateful for the qualities of French wrought iron!

The Saturday morning came, all too quickly for some of us, with the sun up and the aroma of fresh coffee coming from the hotel café. But there was little time to delay – we were to be collected early and driven off through the French countryside in a bus which pulled up at the gates of a fairytale castle. It was a sumptuous place, and once inside, we were taken to – yes, you've guessed it – the restaurant for a five-course lunch.

We worked our way through that with the devotion and determination we rugby men had shown ploughing through the mud of Cardiff or Christchurch, Dublin or Dunedin. Of course, there was the time between leaving the chateau and arriving back at our hotel in Castres when we wouldn't be eating, but Gerard had thought of that. The bus broke the journey halfway and we piled into a *petit auberge* for cognacs at tea-time – just in case we felt a bit thirsty by then, I suppose.

The bed suffered a second severe test as we crashed out on it back at the hotel, but it was to be yet another brief visit to a piece of furniture which we were coming to see as something of a haven from the force-feeding programme. There was just time for a bath and change before the bus picked us up and took us back to the clubhouse we had left in the small hours – for dinner, of course! It was a repeat performance of the previous night, except that this time they really pushed the boat out for their guests. There were eight courses!

In the days when I played rugby, the amount of food we ate was carefully controlled. I know that such standards slip somewhat when you retire but if this was intended to be any sort of preparation for the match the next day, it seemed more like a subtle form of torture.

The culinary bashing went on into the small hours; once more, we staggered home to our beds. The next day at noon, we were at it again – lunch with, would you believe, steak and mashed potatoes with plenty of bottles of red wine. And don't try to say 'No', because everybody was drinking it and enjoying the company. As lunchtime passed, thoughts turned to 'Le match'.

This would not be, as we quickly discovered the next day, just a knock-about game. Indeed, how could it be with some of the people involved – Jo Maso and Mike Gibson at centre outside, Phil Bennett and myself at half-back, with J.P.R. Williams at full-back in the invitation XV which was meeting the French Grand Slam of 1977. Several former French greats were playing for our team, including two of the formidable Spanghero brothers, Claude and Walter, as well as Maso.

There was something else about this game. I was clutching in my hand, metaphorically speaking, a 'Get out of jail' card. I had accepted Gerard's original invitation on the strict condition that I played for just five minutes of the match before coming off. As the food and wine went down during the course of the previous thirty-six hours, I became more and more relieved about that proviso. The way I was starting to feel, I reckoned I was in serious danger of exploding if the feasting and drinking carried on much longer. Certainly, playing a game of rugby on top of it was beginning to look positively dangerous.

But I suppose the one thing nobody could ever accuse me of during my playing career was not being up for the contest, and the whiff of the match in my nostrils again this day was enough to convince me I was, after all, in the finest fettle possible. My five minutes turned into more than an hour. I didn't stay out there because I felt under an obligation. Nobody on that field had anything to prove. It was simply that I was being reminded what a marvellous, magnificent game this continues to be and what fun those who take part in it can have. The skills of all those players were still very much apparent, if somewhat slower than once was the case. It was fabulous to see them do their stuff and be involved again. I couldn't get enough of it. So much so, that when I made a break a long way from the opposition line and headed off downfield, I actually kept running, rather than stopping and looking where to pass. Maureen was apparently sitting in the stand shouting, 'Stop, don't run!'

You might have thought just a few hundred nostalgic souls would have turned up to see this collection of players from yesteryear running around as best they could and trying to play a passable game. Well, almost 20,000 were there and the atmosphere was brilliant. The afternoon's entertainment had started with a juniors' game before the 'veterans' played. We were received regally.

By the time the match finished, it was late on the Sunday afternoon, but there was just time for another spectacular feast to be laid before our bewildered eyes. I doubt whether we did it even half justice before we climbed into the bus and made the hour-long dash back to Toulouse, where we arrived just in time to catch the plane for London.

It had been the most wonderful French experience I'd probably ever known in my entire life. Such occasions set the French, and French rugby, apart. We had experienced not only the most sumptuous food and wines, but on a more personal level, been shown love and affection, not to mention respect, by everyone we had met.

Talking of love and affection, you have to be careful with the French. There is always the potential for, shall we say, a certain degree of misunderstanding. Take the case of my niece Julie and that wonderfully handsome young man who used to be the star of the Toulouse and France teams in the mid-1980s, Denis Charvet.

Today, Julie is happily married to Andre Barnard, a rugby player with the Pontypridd club. Andre, poor fellow, will always be remembered as one of the so-called 'Brive Three', the group alleged to have been involved in certain incidents after Pontypridd's European match against the French club in the Correze, a season or two back. A match full of emotion and controversy spilled over into brawling in a bar in the town later that night with some players from both sides involved. The aftermath filled pages of newspaper space for days afterwards.

Call me biased if you like, but I think Julie is very nice-looking indeed. It seems that view was shared by others, Denis Charvet among them. She came along to Ieuan Evans's testimonial match at Stradey a couple of years ago, and she asked me if I would please get Denis to sign an autograph for her. I duly introduced them, Denis wrote not so much his autograph as a poem and everyone seemed very happy. No more was thought or said about it.

Months later, I received a phone call at home one night from a man with a heavy accent.

'Gareeth, where is Neath?' said the voice.

I thought it was either one of my pals trying to wind me up, or somebody I had met abroad asking for some help in getting to Neath. So I replied politely.

'Well, it's about five miles from Swansea. You go up the valley road and . . .'

'No, no, no,' said the voice. 'Where is Neath, Gareeth?'

'Neath?' I replied.

'Yes, Neath. You remember, Gareeth, I meet Julie at Stradey for Ieuan's match. You introduce me. It is Denis Charvet.'

'Oh, my niece, Julie.'

It transpired that Denis was over with a French TV company for a match, and wanted Julie's number to ask her out for dinner. Anyway, they did meet up and had a pleasant evening. Whenever Denis was in Wales, he would ring her up and they'd try to meet. That happened a few times. Then, one time, after dinner, Julie said she had to go. When Denis asked why, the reply shook him.

'I have to go to my cat.'

He looked at her incredulously and shook his head.

'You live with . . . my cat?' he said, hardly able to get the last two words out.

'Yes,' said Julie, a little surprised herself at why Denis should be so astonished because she had a cat at home. Denis looked even more puzzled.

'Julie, tell me truth. Why you go now?'

'Denis, I love my cat. I have to go back home to him now.'

Denis Charvet had faced some of world rugby's toughest men and withstood some pretty hefty tackles in his time, but Julie's words seemed to have knocked him flat, and she just couldn't understand why. But she had to get off home and that was that. I saw her a few weeks later.

'How did you get on with Denis?' I asked her.

'Well,' she said, 'it was very nice, but he's a funny bloke. We had a lovely evening but then I told him I had to go home to my cat and he went all odd. I think he was in a bit of a huff when I left him.' I knew why as soon as she said it.

'But Julie, I bet Denis thinks you were living with Mike Catt. That's what it was all about,' I said. And that was it! But you couldn't blame Julie – she didn't even know who Mike Catt was!

As the years have gone by, you could have sworn I lived in France. People there seemed always to greet me with such warmth. I am by no means the only player from my era to experience this. I have always felt comfortable with the French players, despite the language barrier, and occasions like Cholley's testimonial have cemented those relationships. To sit with old friends and playing colleagues or opponents around dining tables in, say, Toulouse or Paris, is one of the great pleasures of life. For rugby in France really is something special. There is a camaraderie which continues long after individual players have retired. Indeed, the French seem to revere their golden oldies, former international players, perhaps even more than we do in the British Isles. Their total love of the game, those who played it and what it all means is special.

Events following my first cap against France, at the old Colombes stadium in 1967, took my breath away. You didn't have dinner after the match in Paris – it was always a banquet with nothing but the best. France and Wales were the two dominant countries at that time and although it was ferocious rugby, two hours later it was all friendship, beers, wines, food and a great night together. The French are quick to spot a weakness in an opponent but there was always a general appreciation of each other when our two countries met. Was this, I wondered, the respect ancient warriors had for each other?

I used to have the feeling that other countries' chief intent was to stop us playing. I suppose they felt that if they could do that, they might keep the score down and somehow snatch an unlikely win. But when it came to playing France, you knew you had to perform at your best to stand a chance because their only ambition was to beat you by running you off your feet.

The whole experience of rugby matches in France has always been special. I had a very early taste of it when I was chosen to represent Welsh Schoolboys against their French counterparts at Dijon, on the northern tip of the great Burgundy wine region. Now, with the benefit of hindsight, I can see what a good introduction to future contests with the French it really was.

There was the usual unforgettable meal on the train down to Dijon from Paris, followed by the demands of the game itself. For some reason, I recall, we played about ten minutes extra time before France won, causing us great disappointment, as you can imagine. But our first taste of Ricard doubtless raised spirits and then there was wine at dinner. It was all classically

French, done in style with great taste and skill.

When I became a member of the Cardiff first team, we went down to the Cognac region one year to play matches against La Rochelle and Cognac, two rugby clubs in that enchanting corner of France. The hospitality of the Martell and Hennessy cognac houses, gave me another early introduction to the wider aspects and pleasures of French life.

That visit was an all too rare example of a rugby match in the provinces of France. Usually, we played in Paris and while I loved going to one of the greatest cities in the world, I confess that I wish I'd played more rugby down south, in the real heartland of the French club game. After I retired and visited Toulouse, Castres and other southern towns, I realised how strongly rugby features in French society. I went to Toulouse to report on a France–New Zealand match one year and had a wonderful time meeting old friends like Jo Maso, Jean Pierre Rives and Pierre Villepreux. Eating the traditional local dish, cassoulet, in the Hautes Garonne or Gers regions, washed down with some excellent red wine, is an experience beyond comparison. Seeing rugby folk down there, talking with them in some of the local bars, restaurants and cafés made me realise that Paris, for all its atmosphere, was not the centre of French rugby. It lay in all the towns and villages of the south and west.

Attending a French Club Championship final is one of the great rugby experiences of my life. I saw Toulouse play Castres a few seasons back and it was fantastic, a really special atmosphere. The final is played in Paris now, but go back two or three decades, and it was staged on rota in one of three major cities of the south: Toulouse, Bordeaux or Lyons. For atmosphere, I am told, that was something else. Even in Paris, it is a spectacle to behold. In May 1999, Stade Toulouse beat

Montferrand before 75,000 people at the new Stade de France. Like Twickenham for the English Cup final and, I trust, Cardiff in the years to come for the Welsh Cup final, the vast crowds can be accommodated in these huge new stadia. But it must have been more personal watching a final in one of those three provincial French cities.

Where else did I enjoy my rugby? Well, playing the Irish national side at Lansdowne Road was always the most severe of tests, both on and off the field. Trying to contain the Irish players was as tough as handling the constant pints of Guinness which kept coming at you from all quarters on the Saturday night. I didn't play anywhere else in Ireland very often. Cardiff played the occasional match in Cork, but apart from that, there were all too few times. After I retired, I seemed to go to Ireland more often, especially during the 1980s to commentate on international matches with Bill McLaren. I'd run into lots of the Welsh fans at Cardiff airport on the way. They'd be off to Paris or Edinburgh for the Wales game.

'See you there, Gar,' they'd say.

'I doubt it, boys,' I'd reply. 'I'm off to Dublin for the England game.' And always there was the same response.

'Duw, what you going there for to see that lot then?'

Wherever I went, whether it be Dublin, Edinburgh, Twickenham or even Paris, there would be a game of golf arranged for sometime on the Friday. Quite often, a group of former players would fix up a match somewhere and have a great time. The Robert Paparemborde golf tournament played on one of the best courses in Paris, such as the Nationale or the Racing Club's lovely course at Versailles, is just one such occasion. But you have to watch those French handicaps closely!

As players, we inevitably occupied a narrower corridor.

Although we had more opportunities to see the country we were visiting than players do today, we were pretty much focused on the match, and preparations for it. How many English players, for example, remember much about the Trianon Palace Hotel at Versailles, where they always stayed when they were in Paris for the French match? It was the headquarters of Supreme Allied Commander Dwight Eisenhower in the latter stages of the Second World War. What a privilege, what an opportunity for young men to stay in a place where most of the Allies' top generals met and discussed the assault on Germany in 1944 and early '45.

After I retired, International Rugby Board laws prevented me from going into coaching. I'd written a book and that made me a professional in the eyes of the game's administrators. I admit that the image of myself donning a tracksuit three nights a week at some club up the valleys and running up and down a wet training ground barking orders at players does not fit very comfortably. I could not see myself doing that somehow, but the fact that I was professionalised made it irrelevant anyway.

But I did want to put something back into the game. I said if anyone rang me up and asked me to do something, I would do it. The phone calls never came, perhaps because people realised my position. Doubtless the same happened to Barry John, Gerald Davies, Graham Price and the others.

Wales was not the only country to suffer in this way. In England, the loss of the coaching skills of respected players like Bill Beaumont and Fran Cotton was inestimable. The game as a whole was clearly losing out on a multitude of talent and experience, and eventually the ruling was changed so that players didn't lose their amateur status when they wrote books; but it was too late for me.

Would I have made a good coach? I don't know. There may be no substitute for experience, but experience and a box full of international caps never guaranteed anyone success as a coach in any sport. For a start, you will inevitably be measured by your team. Only in a very few, exceptional cases is a coach likely to enjoy great success with an ordinary group of players.

However, I do feel I could have fulfilled an administrative role, in the way that Colin Meads and Brian Lochore have done in New Zealand, and many former French players have, too. We now have a few former players in Wales who have contributed but not nearly as many as the French.

Perhaps the experience of those who played in my era could have been passed on to a new Welsh generation and helped bridge the gap. Maybe there were roles we could have played in areas such as PR and marketing. But I suspected all along there were a lot of people in Welsh rugby who wanted to prove it wasn't necessarily the players of that era that had made Wales great. Many thought it was the system that was responsible. They had a rude awakening on that score in the years that followed.

The locations may change but not the reception the rugby players of my era receive. I was in Belfast a few years ago, invited to play golf as part of a testimonial for Pat Jennings, that great Northern Ireland goalkeeper. We went out for the evening and found ourselves in a nightclub somewhere outside Newry. When we walked in, we were given a fantastic reception. The atmosphere was as it always seems to be in any Irish bar or nightclub, alive with vibrancy and expectation. There were hundreds of people there. I called the waiter over to where we were sitting and asked for a drink. 'Where would you like it?' said yer man when he returned carrying the bubbly, which by then had been opened. It seemed reasonable enough to say, 'Would you please put it in the ice bucket?' He certainly did that, pouring it literally into the bucket where the contents of a bottle of champagne washed around with a lot of iced water. Kevin Keegan, who was also there, and I crack up every time we see each other and remember that.

Ireland is invariably a place where a smile isn't far from your face. I remember one time when I'd been fishing over on the west coast with Maureen and an old fishing friend, Peter O'Reilly. We drove back to Dublin, intending to have dinner, stay the night and then fly home the next morning. I had a nice bag of fresh fish which I carried proudly into the hotel. I asked them whether they would be so kind as to keep it in the cold store overnight. 'Ah, no problem, sir,' came the reply.

We were in a real rush by the time we checked in because last orders for dinner were at ten and it was close to that time when we finally arrived. I wanted to take a quick shower before dinner after that long drive and they gave me the room key.

'Now, we'll bring your bags up for you, sir,' said the man on the desk. I hesitated, but thought I'd better hurry. I showered and came out into the room, but couldn't find any bags. I rang reception.

'Ah, sorry sir,' said the voice. 'I think you'll be finding your bag outside the room.' And so I did, but when I opened it up in the room to look for a shirt, I pulled out a couple of wet salmon. Soon after, they retrieved my clothes bag from the cold store!

The jokes and fun times are what we remember best, but life can never be only about laughter. The ultimately sad story concerning my friend Jock Turner illustrates the point. Among the things I have enjoyed most in recent years have been my fishing trips to Scotland. I used to go there regularly to fish with

Jock, an old friend of mine from the 1968 British Lions tour of South Africa. J.W.C. Turner of Gala and Scotland played international rugby as a centre three-quarter from 1966 to 1971, appearing against Wales in four of those six seasons. Our respect for each other was supplemented by our shared passion for fishing. When Jock discovered how much I loved it, he invited me up to stay with him at his home in Melrose, near the famous Tweed.

Jock was a man after my own heart. He played rugby to a very high level, but also loved two principal country pursuits – fishing and shooting. Sometimes, as is the case with any friendship, we wouldn't be in touch for a few months. Then, suddenly, the phone would ring and a broad Scottish voice would say, 'Gareth, I'm on the Tweed and the water is rising.' I'd be green with envy, and anxious to get up there to share the pleasure with him as quickly as possible.

One day, I got a call from him and we had a chat. He mentioned that he'd had a frozen shoulder and remarked on how painful it had been. He'd had it for some months and it didn't seem to be making very much progress. To Jock, full movement in the arms and shoulders was essential for casting the fly. I already had a standing invitation for a day's fishing near Perth and instead of making the five-hundred mile drive in one go, Jock suggested travelling a day or so earlier, breaking the journey at his house and then going on, after a day's fishing with him. It seemed a marvellous idea.

When I got there, he told me that the shoulder pain was pretty bad and he was having trouble sleeping. It seemed strange it couldn't be sorted out. Nevertheless, we went off the next morning, a beautiful, bright day I recall, and we began to fish. It wasn't long before I was into a fish. The salmon was duly landed, accompanied by the banter and lighthearted comments plus torrent of abuse that is very much the way of fishermen.

We'd taken a bottle of wine with us down to the river, and Pat, Jock's wife, had made some lovely sandwiches. We retired to the fishing hut beside the river for our lunch, and whiled away a couple of hours exchanging tales from days gone by. It was delightful; quality time you'd call it. We were going to go back to the fishing later, when the sun was off the water. But Jock never made it. We went home for some tea and to rest for a while. Pat and I were talking, relaxing, when Jock collapsed and died of a massive heart attack right in front of our eyes. Jock, a dearly beloved friend, was only forty-eight. He and his family had been charming and hospitable; his home was open to me. He was a fine man and a great friend whom I still miss to this day.

It has been a privilege to know people like Jock. What concerns me about the game today is that we may have created a whole new generation coming into the sport who know only about two points on a Saturday, not two pints. I fear the game will have little room for making friends in future, for the type of special camaraderie that has underpinned it all. People have asked me if rugby would lose anything if it lost that. My reply is, 'Well, that *was* rugby.' What other sport can you play with such effort, emotion and aggression with a real possibility of injury yet forget it within an hour and have a few beers and lots of fun with your opponents? Very few, I suspect.

I'd like to think that any player wearing a Welsh international jersey will always feel every bit as much pride and passion as we did. He should understand the history and tradition that go before him in wearing that shirt. It has never been, and never will be in my eyes, just another jersey. It is the jersey of our nation. Every player fortunate enough to be asked to wear it should do so with enormous pride. For me, standing there while the national anthem played, wearing that shirt, produced the greatest emotion I ever knew in my sporting life. The feeling of pride was immense, the most fantastic feeling in all the world. Every time it was the same. But perhaps in Wales we went through an era where many people who didn't deserve an international cap, got one. Maybe that further undermines the cachet, the exclusivity of an international cap. In those years of turmoil for Welsh rugby, caps began to be handed out like confetti. I regretted that because it must have devalued the prestigious concept of a Welsh cap. Certainly, awarding caps for a match against the Barbarians, a quite ridiculous decision, brought a Welsh cap closer to ridicule than it can ever have been before.

It was interesting to hear David Campese lambasting the modern Australian players, saying they didn't have either the skill or commitment that becoming a Wallaby should always entail. He felt they didn't understand the pride involved in wearing an Australian jersey. You could hardly call Campo an arch tradition-alist, a boiled shirt, as we say, but hearing him speak in such terms, I did begin to wonder whether the modern player around the world does understand the value of playing for his country; or whether, to use a phrase very much in vogue these days, it isn't terribly cool to get too excited about winning a cap.

But you can only speak of your own experiences and for me, rugby truly created the pleasure principle. I am proud and happy to say that it has remained with me for all of my life.

CHAPTER TWELVE

The Barbarians

As a club, it is unique. It has no paying members, doesn't own a ground and doesn't even possess a clubhouse. Just what sort of a club is without those basic requirements, you might wonder. Well, for myself and countless other rugby players past and present, this rugby club holds a truly special place in our hearts. But then, the Barbarians always have been different.

I must have been asked thousands of times why it is so special, why it means so much to us. I think the answer is that the Barbarians have always epitomised a certain style on and off the field. They offered a type of rugby which instantly appealed to everyone, players and spectators, because it was free-flowing, creative, attacking rugby without the intensity of an international match.

Some have said to me, 'Well, Wales played rugby like that in the 1970s. So what was different about the Barbarians?' Probably the sheer enjoyment factor – we could do it without the knowledge in the back of our minds that a mistake or two might cost us defeat in an international. Of course, that discipline is all part of international rugby and what makes it special, but there is no doubt it was delightful to attack teams, trying to use your skills and those of your team-mates, without having that potent factor of having to win the match in the back of your minds. Not that too many Barbarians games I played in were lighthearted, irrelevant games in which it didn't matter whether you won or lost, particularly when you were playing the likes of New Zealand, Australia or South Africa. In 1973, for example, the Barbarians side I played for against New Zealand had a nucleus of players from the successful 1971 British Lions who had toured in New Zealand. Therefore, there was an expectation that we would play like the Lions had done.

Nevertheless, even though we did our utmost to win those traditional end-of-tour fixtures, we knew that entertainment and quality rugby were the priority. That has always been the creed of the Barbarians club. To this day, it has remained in my view a breath of fresh air away from the pressures and often negative approach of domestic and international rugby. Playing rugby football with spontaneity has a rich appeal. Only the Barbarians have consistently been able to deliver, because they have remained faithful to their beliefs and because they operate outside the confines of Test match rugby.

Now may be the era of professional rugby, but we were professional in our approach and preparation. We felt the pressure of expectation, particularly in Wales. Therefore, the opportunity to play games with or against the Barbarians always found favour with the players because it did take you briefly out of that context. There was a sense of freedom.

The Barbarians were founded in 1890, and have always been

renowned for the quality of their rugby, determined to demonstrate the finest attributes of the game. Players through the years have regarded it as an honour to wear that coveted Barbarians tie, to don the famous black and white shirt, especially those who had perhaps not quite been good enough to play international rugby, or young players who had yet to win an international cap. In both cases, the experience of playing alongside established internationals, many of whom might have been household names, was always warmly appreciated. I know – I have talked to so many players who have been through that unique experience. Several players who had given sterling service to the game in one way or another but might not necessarily have played international rugby, were awarded a Barbarians jersey. They appreciated that gesture more than most could say. Conversely, Barbarians games often served as a launchpad for some rugby careers that were to become most distinguished on the international fields of the world.

I first represented the Barbarians in 1967 when we played the touring New Zealanders in the end-of-tour fixture at Twickenham. Of course, I was never chosen for the Barbarians party for their full Easter tour of South Wales, an institution that had begun back in 1925 with matches against Penarth on Good Friday, Cardiff on Easter Saturday, Swansea on Easter Monday and Newport the following day. This tradition lasted until the 1980s when it sadly began to erode. It is one of the few regrets I have that I could never be available for that full Easter tour because I played for Cardiff against the Barbarians in the traditional Easter Saturday fixture. Those players who were chosen always said the Easter tour was special for the friendships you made, the camaraderie and the singing and drinking which often went on long into the night.

I did play once for the Barbarians during their 1968 Easter tour, because Roger Pickering, the Yorkshire and England scrum-half who was on that Easter tour, was injured and I was asked if I would play against Swansea on the Monday. I didn't need to think twice. One of the reasons was that directly opposite me that day would be the Swansea and Wales scrum-half of the earlier 1960s, Clive (D.C.T.) Rowlands, who later coached Wales. That proved to be an education in itself. I'd just won my first couple of caps for Wales but it was a case of the boy against the man. I thought I'd give him bit of cheeky lip at the first scrum.

'Come on, Rowlands, get on with it,' I called out, as he went to pick up the ball for the scrum feed. Clive stopped in his tracks, turned round and said, 'Hey, you. You're not old enough to talk to me like that yet.' Perhaps I'd unsettled him by my cheek. When the ball came out of the back of the Swansea scrum, I dived between Clive's legs, got hold of it and was awarded a try. He retorted, 'Cheeky little bugger.' I don't think he's ever forgotten it, either.

That summed up some Barbarians matches. They were played with a real competitive edge and yet you had time for good-natured little asides like that, moments of fun that would have been unthinkable in the cauldron of international rugby.

That day at Swansea held another attraction for me. In the Barbarians side were the French pair, Jean Gachassin, a wizard of a little outside-half known at that time as the 'Peter Pan' of rugby, and the full-back Claude Lacaze. Claude's last-minute penalty kick at goal for France against Wales in the Championship match at Cardiff a couple of months earlier, had just drifted wide, allowing Wales to squeeze home 9–8. That was a match made famous by Stuart Watkins' interception try for Wales.

I was twenty and regarded it as a huge incentive to wear the Barbarians shirt in such company. Jean and myself operated on the basis of a little French, a little English; rugby was our common language. There may have been a bit of 'Mon Dieu, Gareth', or 'Oh no, Jean' from time to time, but I think we both knew what we wanted to achieve that day. When the Barbarians came visiting, Cardiff would draw a huge crowd, around 25,000, for one of the highlights of our season.

One of the Barbarians games I played in that had a unique flavour was the 1977 Queen's Silver Jubilee match against the British Lions of that year. The Barbarians chose an all French back row, that fantastic combination of Jean Pierre Rives, Jean Claude Skrela and Jean Pierre Bastiat, the tall, powerful No. 8. I'd played against them several times for Wales and knew from personal experience, having been a target of their attention, what a formidable unit they were. To have them on the same side for a change, was wonderful; a lot more comfortable too. I'd achieved a bit in rugby by then but despite all that, the thrill of playing in the same side as that French back row was beyond price.

So much for glorious pasts. What of the future? I am convinced the Barbarians have a future. They must have a future because without them this game will be an awful lot poorer. Whether the club needs to change tack or not is a question that will be answered in the fullness of time. Once we come up with a sensible structure to the season, I hope that provision will be made for a few Barbarians matches here and there. The players of the future will then discover the pure pleasure and enjoyment that we have all derived from the

Barbarians throughout this century.

For a start, I see no reason why we cannot retain the traditional fixture against the touring side. It may be difficult with an overseas team that comes in for just a one-off Test match, as Australia did to England in autumn 1998. But if a touring team is in Britain perhaps visiting only two of the four countries, there ought to be the opportunity to conclude their visit with a match against the Barbarians at a venue they have not visited on the trip. From the Barbarians' point of view, that match could not be the sole game on its fixture list. That would be too much of a luxury. So what chances are there of other fixtures? I know that Cardiff would welcome further contact with them. I don't think anyone pretends that a full Easter tour of South Wales is possible any longer, but a one-off match against a Barbarians team able to select players of sufficient quality would still draw big crowds to Cardiff, especially if it were on Easter Saturday, the traditional occasion for the game.

The same applies to Leicester who traditionally meet the Barbarians just after Christmas. That, too, is a fixture which rugby supporters show no sign of wanting to end, despite the difficulty the Barbarians have had in recent seasons attracting enough good players to their ranks. There's the rub – the Baabaas can only continue to delight and attract rugby supporters if they can put out a side worthy of the occasion. When that began to get difficult, the Easter tour of South Wales was undermined and then stopped.

It is impossible to see a future for the Barbarians if coaches cannot glimpse the wider picture, and refuse point blank to release their best players for any matches played by the Barbarians. Of course, it is easy to understand their concerns if they have a lot of injuries or are involved in a major match.

For example, over Easter 1999 four clubs in England were involved in the semi-finals of the Tetley's Bitter Cup. It would have been unreasonable to expect Richmond, Newcastle, Wasps or Gloucester to release any of their top players. But if the Barbarians had been playing, would it have been so difficult for clubs like Harlequins or Northampton to release a few players for the day?

I cannot believe the clubs of England, Wales, Ireland and Scotland cannot find a couple of dates in the course of a year to release one each of their leading players. You know the old saying, 'Where there's a will, there's a way'. I certainly believe the players would welcome the chance to step away, however briefly, from the pressures of competitive club rugby each week.

One problem is that the Six Nations Championship has been pushed back towards spring, so that international players seem to be involved with that level of rugby much later in the season. The Barbarians fixtures at Easter took place almost as a season finale, but that wouldn't be possible today, with the climax of the Six Nations still to be played. Any Barbarians fixture played before the end of the Six Nations would mean difficulty in recruiting the best players from those countries involved. Leading players are what the Barbarians have to have to survive. Their great tradition is such that anything much less would be seen immediately as something of a poor relation.

In France where the Barbarians concept has grown in strength in recent years, they do not attempt to play many fixtures. Now and again, a French Barbarians side plays a match and they seem able to attract good players. It is my great wish that we could do something similar here. If we can't, perhaps the example of the New Zealand Barbarians is one that we should follow. As I have mentioned elsewhere, their method of playing matches for charity and helping at schools, is something that we should examine. One thing is certain – we must not let this wonderful concept, this great club, simply wither away and die. We have too much to lose.

The Barbarians themselves may have to move with the times to survive. Their tradition of never paying their players has been laudable, but that may have to change. There probably has to be some reward in the modern era. If that is the price for saving the club, I would think it worth paying.

Are these the dying words of an old dinosaur? Is this wish to maintain so worthy a tradition the lament of someone living in the past? That's for others to say, but I hope not. It is just that I have experienced the all-round education the matches of this club brought me, the comradeship, the friendship, the great pleasure of playing rugby in this style. I believe that all of these things are worth fighting to preserve, and I am sure that is not solely my view. If the death knell does sound for this fine institution, I hope the game has thought through the wider implications of its demise, and realises what a great part of its tradition it would be losing.

There have been so many outstanding Barbarians occasions down the years, but it seems that, inevitably, everyone is drawn to 1973 and the fixture against Ian Kirkpatrick's touring All Blacks. They called it 'The club's greatest day' and I suppose in many respects it was for the sheer quality of rugby played and the impression it left. It was a special occasion, a match that truly caught fire, yet I have to admit I remain astonished by the on-going level of interest in the game. In March 1999, twenty-six years after that game of rugby, I stood up to speak at a function in Leicester, having been introduced to warm and generous applause as 'The man who scored that fabulous try for the Barbarians'. A few weeks earlier, I had attended a business conference in Hampshire and had no sooner walked into the room than complete strangers were coming up to me and saying, 'Gareth, tell us about that try.'

They didn't mean the kick and chase effort against Scotland at the Arms Park when I ended up covered in the red shale and my mother, sitting in the stand, thought I'd cut myself from head to foot! They weren't referring to the one I scored against Ireland at Cardiff in 1973, when we needed a score to squeeze home by 16 points to 12; nor were they asking about any I managed for the British Lions on tours in 1968, 1971 or 1974. It was just *that* try, and *that* match. I am always happy to oblige and pass on my memories of a wonderful day for the game.

If I have enjoyed recalling it, and I admit I have, it has been to give people an insight into how many things could have gone wrong during the move. When I see the try replayed on television, usually at some official function, I still get a buzz from watching it. Even after all these years, I'm never quite sure whether I'm going to get there each time!

If it were on *Question of Sport* and they stopped the frame when Phil Bennett first got the ball running back close to his own line, the query 'What happened next?' might be hard to answer if you didn't know. I doubt whether many would have said a try was scored at the other end of the field, certainly not against the New Zealanders. I think my answer would have been, 'Phil Bennett gets splattered.' That was one reason why I was shouting for Phil to get rid of the ball by kicking it into touch. Now there's a confession for you; the try some have called the greatest ever scored might never have happened if I'd got my grubby little hands on it at the start of the movement.

Some people have said it could never be called the most fantastic try scored because it wasn't in a Test match. Maybe not, but it was still against the New Zealanders. They never play a match just for a bit of fun. Creating and scoring such a try against them give it an added flavour, to my way of thinking. Although it happened all those years ago and was over in a flash, it is almost as though the moment is frozen in time and forever repeated.

When the ball went back to Phil, it had already been in play for some little while. I was gasping for air and wanted play to stop so as to get a bit of a breather. But when Phil did the complete opposite to what I and most of our team expected and probably hoped he would do, namely produce a comfortable clearing kick to touch, the play suddenly flared up again. Immediately after Phil's dancing side-steps, I remember JPR's head almost being taken off in a tackle. But when John Pullin got the ball, I had to make some effort to let those guys come past me. By this time, I was quietly cursing, thinking to myself, 'What are they doing now?' But the noise level of the crowd was rising and was lifting the whole stadium, players and spectators. Normally, when you play in a major match, you are not aware of the noise down on the ground but I was this time.

By the time I turned around and was facing downfield, three or four passes had occurred in the movement and play had gone from near our line to thirty or forty yards downfield. I knew I had better run hard to catch it up, although there was no thought whatever in my mind that we would score and I might be the one to touch down. It still seemed too far out for that to happen. I suspected the ball would go to ground very soon and as I was scrum-half, it was my responsibility to be there close to it, if and when that happened. As Tom

David took the ball on following John Dawes' short burst, I found I was really having to turn up the speed to get near to the movement. This was probably the key to my eventual involvement because by the time I was just getting close to where the play was, I was sprinting flat out. I could not have received the ball at a better moment because I just hit the line with maximum speed and impact, and that pace took me away up the touchline.

When I caught the ball, it was almost like an interception because I knew John Bevan was waiting outside me and Joe Karam was sizing him up. So I shouted to Derek Quinnell in Welsh, 'Throw it here.' I still remember the thrill, the surge of adrenalin as I took the pass and hit the gain line before sweeping around Karam.

What do you think about in those split seconds? Was I contemplating a glorious touchdown at the end of a superb movement? No, not at all. The only thing in my mind was whether my hamstrings would stand up to the all-out sprinting I was now doing. I prayed they wouldn't seize up in that mad dash for the corner.

Whether there was time for me to run the last few yards to the line, I wouldn't know even now. The reason I dived was that I remembered something Bill Samuel had taught me at school, years earlier. See what I mean about strange, unexpected thoughts going through your mind at such moments? Bill said that when you dive for the line, it makes it more difficult for the defending side to stop you. I knew that the cover was coming across and was closing me down fast, but I was too scared to look to see just how close they were. In the event, of course, I think it was Grant Batty who managed to collar me but my momentum was enough to get me there.

I had scored some important tries before that day, and I was lucky enough to get some others in the times that followed, but I never scored another try to such deafening applause. The noise was enough to burst your eardrums. I felt a mixture of emotions. There was probably the sense that something outstanding had occurred, for the buzz around the ground said it all. There was also in my mind a sense of disbelief that such a try could be scored against the New Zealanders of all people.

It had all happened so quickly I didn't know how good a movement it had been. All I could take on board at that stage was that we had scored a try from one end of the field to the other in the first four minutes. Another thought came to me as I was walking back before the conversion and that was how dreadful our preparation had been for the game that week. We'd had virtually no time to come together and the training in Penarth had been shocking. Whatever we tried went wrong. I doubt whether there could have been a worse dress rehearsal; there had been dropped passes all over the place. Then another thought came to me – 'Why couldn't it have been in the last minute, not at the beginning of the match?' But of course, I was very happy that we had scored such a try because it lifted the whole game. The rest of the match was played at an extraordinary pace with magnificent rugby from both sides. People do acknowledge even today that it was an outstanding game.

The Barbarians' philosophy of playing open, exciting rugby perhaps put added pressure on us that day. Of course, there had been great moments before in Barbarians rugby history: Wilson Whineray's special moment at the end of the New Zealand tour in 1964, the chairing off the field of the Springbok captain Avril Malan at the end of the South Africans' tour in 1961. We all felt the pressure of expectation from the crowd. Also it was the first opportunity for British spectators to witness the nucleus of the victorious 1971 Lions team. Pride of performance and the opportunity to lower the colours of the touring team came into it as further incentives.

Who knows the reason but things gelled that day and that try set it on its way. It was one of the best games I ever played in and we produced some outstanding rugby for the best part of that first half. Whatever we tried to do we seemed to succeed. There was the distinct feeling that at 17–0 up at half-time, New Zealand were a little fortunate to be still in the game. We had missed other scoring opportunities we probably should have taken. But from my experience of having played against New Zealand on several occasions, I was well aware of their capacity to soak up pressure and never lie down. They duly turned on the power in the second half and all but levelled within twenty minutes of the re-start.

What we achieved overall in that match was an accurate portrayal of the way the Lions had played in 1971. Carwyn James had been invited to be honorary coach and he passed on comments to the Barbarians for a couple of days beforehand. His message was simple: 'Boys, believe in yourselves, look for the opportunities.' I still remember so many things about that day. Phil Bennett's audacious first move to start the try, David Duckham's wonderful running from deep, the control and slick passing along the line of John Dawes and Mike Gibson and the powerful running of John Bevan. Also, there was the reminder that the value of quick ball never diminishes. It was all reminiscent of that tour to New Zealand in 1971.

What that game did was raise the profile of British rugby, and the buzz during and after it was unbelievable. Whether I think it was the best match ever or not is irrelevant. What does matter is the impact it had on generations of players and spectators. I certainly played in more important matches, more meaningful games, but such is the standing of New Zealand that any opportunity to beat them has to be significant. As a Welshman, winning in Paris in 1971 against a great French side to help win the Grand Slam might have been of greater importance, but not even that had the impact the Barbarians game has had. Wales won 9–5 and it could have been 39–35. It was a match full of wonderful open rugby, but only the diehards who were there that day will really remember it.

What helped that 1973 match between the Barbarians and New Zealand enter the folklore of the game was television. People could see it, witness it all instantly. It was a fine game filled with exciting rugby that I'll never forget. But perhaps the more you talk about it, the less you understand why it is remembered so much more than any other game. All I do know is that memories and recollections of it all seem as clear today as they did the day after it was played. There are precious few matches of which you can say the same in rugby's long history.

CHAPTER THIRTEEN

Professionalism: The Background

A nd so we come to the great topic of our time in rugby football, one that has caused, and I suspect will continue to cause, more headlines, make more waves and create more soul-searching than any other the game has known for perhaps a hundred years. The debate concerning professionalism rages on, in a bewildering multiplicity of forms. It is regarded by some in the game today as its saviour, by others as its ruination. It has polarised opinions, created deep rifts and, at the same time, given considerable pleasure, depending upon individual perceptions of its merits or evils.

Before the game was declared open in the late summer of 1995, it was the worst-kept secret in the world that some clubs were flouting the amateur laws and giving players money or, as the quaint old phrase in the amateur code said, reward in kind. Some could afford to, others couldn't. Of course, it was always denied that such payments existed but it became obvious there was a considerable amount of reward being given to some players. One coach told me years ago that when he approached a certain player as to the possibility of him joining that club, the player asked, 'How much?'

'We don't pay money but we might be able to get a local company to provide a car through sponsorship,' he was told.

'That's no good,' the player apparently replied. 'I've already been offered two cars, one for myself and another for the wife, by so-and-so club.'

It was always impossible to verify the truth of these stories but the old saying, 'there's no smoke without fire' seemed a reliable indicator. Besides, the late Clem Thomas revealed in 1996, when he wrote his book *The History of the British Lions*, that when he'd been selected for the 1955 Lions tour to South Africa, the club had given him what he called 'the handsome sum' of £50. Strictly speaking, of course, that professionalised him. But no one worried too much about things like that, even in those far off days.

So when news came through in late August 1995 that the game had been declared open, I was hardly knocked down with shock. It was a *fait accompli*, as I saw it. To preserve the dignity and integrity of the sport, there seemed little choice. But it was not the players who had dragged the game to the verge of professionalism. I attribute that to the sport's authorities, those in charge of the individual unions who had welcomed big business into rugby with open arms to take money off them in ever increasing amounts. Once they had set in motion that trend, then the days of amateur rugby union at the highest levels were always numbered, in my view.

Every major match of any kind had become associated with sponsors because the unions wanted that. There was the British Gas international in Cardiff, the Royal Bank international in Scotland, the Save & Prosper international at Twickenham and the Digital international over in Dublin. Even the University match between Oxford and Cambridge, a fixture which was really the embodiment of amateurism, was sponsored by the Bowring group.

Now I have never had anything against such companies. I fully accept that their monies have contributed enormously to the good health of the whole game. But equally, I always felt it would be impossible to bring all that money into rugby and keep it amateur. Some officials, such as England's RFU secretary Dudley Wood, insisted it could be done, but most people considered it would lead only to one outcome – professionalism. It is therefore with much wry amusement that I sometimes hear officials bemoaning the loss of the old days and an amateur game.

The game could not continue in its old ways. It had become a contradiction in terms, rigidly amateur in the eyes of officialdom in the northern hemisphere, embracing professionalism, if not overtly then certainly covertly, in the southern hemisphere. Something had to give, and it did.

When Rupert Murdoch paid the southern hemisphere nations South Africa, New Zealand and Australia a combined fee of approximately $550 million at the time of the 1995 World Cup for broadcast rights for a new Tri-Nations competition, then everyone in the world with brains to use realised that the old game was finished. It could no longer continue to make a pretence of amateurism.

Long before the deed was done allowing rugby union to go professional, I remember discussing the problems with some leading officials in the game. This was probably as much as twenty-five or more years ago, but I suggested to them that some form of financial compensation should be introduced, solely for the purpose of overcoming the difficulties for players presented by overseas tours.

Employers had funded players making tours abroad for too long and it was obvious the system had to change. My idea was that if the unions did not want to give money to the player himself, then they should make some financial contribution to his employer for the period he would be away. Had financial recompense been available, for example, it is quite possible I would have changed my mind and made myself available for the 1977 British Lions tour of New Zealand. But, as I said earlier in this book, I felt that with a young family to support, I could not expect my employer to give me another thirteen or fourteen weeks off, just to make yet another tour. It wasn't fair on them. The union was profiting, I was having a great time – and my employer was funding it all.

With an increasing number of national tours being arranged apart from the usual Lions tour every four years, most summers began to be filled with an overseas trip. To expect players to be away from their jobs for weeks on end every summer, was asking the impossible.

But, as with so many reasonable and sensible ideas that were put to rugby's respective unions, they would not listen. I am not saying it would have solved every problem in the game, but at least it would have demonstrated an awareness of one of the difficulties facing people in the sport. As it was, the committees were clinging onto their amateur ethos, but conveniently over-looking the fact that they had opened the floodgates and allowed millions of pounds to pour into the sport.

Worst still, some ignorant people trotted out what I considered that grossly offensive line in response to players' difficulties concerning time off for tours. 'You don't have to go if you don't want to' was the retort. But what sort of an answer was that? Here were people putting more and more demands on players, not just tours (I think I saw only one full summer in Wales during my playing career) but also expecting us to train with the threat that if we didn't turn up we wouldn't be selected, yet they were still trying to hang onto the pretence that this was a wholly amateur sport. I can't speak for other players but towards the end of my playing career, I had become involved with rugby every night of the week. You had to give that kind of commitment and still hold down a job, plus, for those who had families, find time for them too. It was becoming an impossible situation.

Given this state of affairs, I could not see how the guardians of the game could look themselves in the mirror and say 'This game is amateur'. Surely it would have helped if the International Board had realised that the demands on players were excessive, and provided a central pool of money to go to his employers. I am sure my employer, Jack Hamer, would have been satisfied with that.

In a sense, the game lost out in every way when the administrators refused to face reality. Firstly, it was obvious they were only delaying the inevitable. Secondly, the sport's credibility suffered given the obvious discrepancies and thirdly, it meant weaker teams set off for overseas tours. In 1974, for example, the Lions toured South Africa without Gerald Davies, David Duckham and Mike Gibson, although the latter did eventually join the tour halfway through. In 1978, Wales went to Australia without several key players.

By then, the sport had come within a whisker of a major schism through the ambitions of a business entrepreneur. David Lord's projected rugby circus was intended to be the first of two big sporting heists by Australian businessmen. Kerry Packer's, in cricket, came off; David Lord's in rugby did not. But people have never realised how close that came to creating a huge problem in the modern game.

What Lord sought to do was to buy up almost all the leading international rugby players of the world, set up a tour and play matches in various rugby locations around the globe. He reasoned that the support, both in terms of crowds at matches and also from sponsors and TV, would be strong enough to run a successful commercial operation.

On the face of it, the concept was entirely workable. There would have been, for want of a better phrase, a sort of travelling circus of international rugby players. They would perhaps have played a match in Cape Town, then gone on for another in Durban and then a third in Johannesburg or Pretoria. After that, following a suitable break, they would have arrived in Australia and played a series of games there between teams comprising the most talented players in the world game who had signed up. After that, they could perhaps have gone to New Zealand and then to Argentina before doing something similar in the northern hemisphere rugby-playing nations of the world.

Lord and his people could see the potential of the sport, and his moves towards creating a breakaway of most of the world's top players set alarm bells ringing. In the end, it failed because too many players were uncertain, although anyone being completely dismissive of it would have been foolish.

There was big money on offer. And if it had come to fruition, it is very likely I would have joined it. It would have helped make me financially secure for the rest of my life. At a time when I was thinking about a family and buying a house, it would have been very useful. I had played the game at the highest level for some years, represented Wales and the Lions. Already, by that stage, I was starting to see these aspects of rugby which I felt were not right, yet administrators were refusing to address them or to confront reality.

Anyone in high office who smiled smugly at the news that Lord's circus had collapsed and that therefore the impetus for change had been lost, perhaps forever, was simply deluding themselves. Because the fact was, the pressure for professional rugby was building inexorably. You could see even several years back, that this just had to lead to professionalism. There was no other way for the game to go.

Each country had its own difficulties. For example, Australia was facing stiff opposition for players and spectators from rugby league. League has always been a stronger sport in Australia than union; it was well supported and full of excellent footballers. Many players who started out in rugby union in that country ended up in league; lured not just by the money but the excitement and quality of football being played in the professional ranks. Many made outstanding careers for themselves, too, such as Russell Fairfax and Ricky Stuart, two great former union players. In Britain, too, a large number of Welsh players and not a few Englishmen headed north to play league, although comparatively few made the cross-over into league from Scotland or Ireland. So it was Welsh teams in particular who were being stripped of their most talented players. It had become a serious problem for rugby union in my country, because the Welsh pool of talent was much smaller than the English one.

But it was not just the pressure from rugby league in both Australia and England that helped finally to burst the dam of amateurism, but also the alarming inconsistencies associated with the old code.

In 1983, the British Lions toured New Zealand. It was to be an ill-fated tour, for the Test series was lost 4–0. But those who made the trek to the land of the long white cloud, were confronted by the startling sight of members of the All Black squad advertising products on national television! It wasn't so much slipping a couple of things in through the backdoor of the house named amateurism, as someone driving a coach and horses right through the front door and doing their best to demolish the entire structure.

Andy Haden, that second row forward who was the bane of the administrators' lives, advertised some vehicle and, in another appearance, advised viewers to read all about the Test match the next day, straight from the horse's mouth, in the Sunday newspaper he wrote for.

I was sitting in a lounge bar somewhere in New Zealand with Bill Beaumont. I looked at Bill and he looked back at me in stunned disbelief. Bill and I had written books, and been banned from the game as a consequence because we had professionalised ourselves, according to the game's guardians. Yet here was a present-day player making television adverts, writing a newspaper column and, it seemed, doing whatever he wished, with complete impunity. But Haden wasn't the only one. Andy Dalton was shown on his farm south of Auckland, putting a four-wheel-drive vehicle through its paces and recommending it to viewers. Dalton, like Haden, played in every Test in that Lions series.

These were blatant examples of what was happening across the southern hemisphere, yet no one in charge of the IRB either felt inclined or confident enough to do the slightest thing about it. Andy Haden had put 'rugby player' in his passport, on the line asking for job details. The authorities hesitated and then did nothing. In fairness to them, it was a very difficult challenge set by Haden. Answering 'rugby player' when asked your occupation meant the authorities were put in a quandary, as I'm sure wily old Andy would have known! Could those charged with administering the game worldwide have succeeded in banning Haden because of his so-called profession? It would have been different perhaps had he tried to pretend that earning money from rugby was a secondary employment. Then, maybe they could have argued that it was not his proper job. But as it was, it seemed hard to believe a court would ban a player from the game for earning his living legally. Which is doubtless the conclusion those in charge came to.

By then, I think everyone knew it was simply a question of time before the whole issue of so-called amateurism in rugby would be addressed and probably ended. Some still manned the barricades, like Dudley Wood, who insisted it would not happen. Not while he was there, anyway. But the problem was only going to intensify. It would not just go away as people like Wood hoped, once Haden had hung up his boots in 1985. Amateurism was in its dying days, the pretence could not continue very much longer, and rightly so.

Two years later, the first Rugby World Cup was staged, co-hosted by Australia and New Zealand. Once again, visitors to New Zealand were presented with the extraordinary sight of the All Black wing John Kirwan advertising on TV, together with his father whom, it was said, was receiving money, not John. And perhaps he was. I saw this hypocrisy as the beginning of the end. I knew then, for certain, that what had become something of a sham of amateurism in certain parts of the world, was going to come tumbling down. I had no problem if Kirwan or anyone else earned something from outside activities associated with the sport because of the tremendous efforts they were putting in. It was unfair not to reward them.

It was on the southern hemisphere's conscience whether they wanted to bend the rules or turn a blind eye to what was going on. But people certainly weren't getting away with it very much in the northern hemisphere. Yet, despite the fierce debate which by now had become a worldwide topic of conversation in sporting circles, nothing happened. Virtually no one was thrown out of the game for professionalising themselves, and no one changed the rules to allow players to exploit commercial opportunities, thus maintaining the principle that they weren't paid to play.

Another factor around the end of the 1980s hastened the increasing reality of professionalism in a game still trying to call itself amateur. The setting up of leagues meant the entire attitude to rugby at club level had to be re-assessed. No longer was this a sport played by people chiefly with a sense of fun, or even simply to test their competitive and physical qualities against others in a series of friendlies (however fiercely contested). Leagues meant prizes, financial rewards for clubs, or the threat of relegation and decline if they didn't compete. This meant players were expected to prepare as professionally as possible. All this was but the shortest of strides away from full-blown professionalism. Indeed, the only link that remained in the game to amateurism was the fact that the players were not being paid. Yet charges to watch international and even club matches were increasing, sponsorship sums were rocketing and money was beginning to wash like a tidal wave through the game.

Anyone who believed this gross anomaly could continue was deluding themself. How could you ask players to spend all this time, training and playing so much and attending training camps without monetary reward? Their careers were suffering, employers were becoming irritated.

If my contemporaries thought the demands had begun to get heavy near the end of our playing careers towards the end of the 1970s, then by the 1990s this was something else. The pressures on the players had been taken to another level, and paying them, openly and honestly, was inevitably going to come.

In 1993 came a seminal moment. To help celebrate the South Africans' return to the fold of international rugby following the lifting of apartheid and their imminent Test match against the Wallabies, the Australian Rugby Union decided to hold a gala dinner in Sydney. At home in Wales, I opened my post one morning to find an invitation to attend this event, followed by another letter from a PR company asking me to be a guest at the Test match. Further investigations revealed that many other former players had also been invited, among them Colin Meads and Wilson Whineray of New Zealand, Morne du Plessis of South Africa, Jacques Fouroux and Jean Pierre Rives of France and David Duckham of England, to mention just a few.

It was a miserable offer. We had to get ourselves to Heathrow airport, be wined and dined in style in business class during the long flight down to Sydney, be ferried to one of that lovely city's top hotels and then attend a sparkling banquet a few nights later at a leading hotel. I suppose someone has to undertake these arduous tasks! We, of course, were invited with all expenses paid. Others at the dinner, it soon transpired, were paying $1000 a ticket for the privilege of being there, which raised a few eyebrows.

But not nearly as many as when the MC, having reminded everyone on the big night that the entire event was live on television (which helped explain the high levels of sponsorship), said that every dollar raised would go to the Australian rugby union squad which was facing the South Africans a few days later.

We former players looked at each other and said: 'Did we really hear what we think we have just heard?' For there was no mention of a Trust fund or anything of the kind. And you certainly didn't have to be a mathematician to work out how much money was being raised. No expenses were to be taken out of it. The fact was, a huge pot of gold was going straight into the coffers of the Aussie rugby squad.

The following day, I talked with a very senior administrator of the Australian Rugby Union and voiced my concerns as to whether I'd misunderstood what it had all been about.

'Not at all, mate,' was his cheerful reply. 'And I wonder what they are going to say at Twickenham about that?'

The Australians' attitude was simply, 'This is what we are doing because it's the only way we can keep our players.' And so they went ahead with it. Yet, officially, rugby union was still an amateur sport, with strict rules and punishments for any Union found to be flouting the code's amateur regulations. But it seemed there could always be a way around any such laws.

As the 1995 World Cup approached, another Australian, Ross Turnbull, was looking to sign up most of the world's leading players in another proposed rugby circus. This was a modern-day equivalent of the David Lord proposal and, like Lord's, it came within a whisker of fulfilment. It is said that, but for the role of just one or two very senior figures among the world's best players who wavered on their alleged original commitment, the whole venture would have succeeded.

I knew this one was also for real, because again I saw genuine contracts. Once more, the administrators of the sport had no idea just how close it was to taking place and splitting the international game. I understand that some players had already put their names to contracts. Had it happened, it would have removed almost all the top strata from the sport, put rugby union into disarray at the highest level and taken, in my estimation, at least two years for the game to recover. The entire club game in most countries would have been devoid of class players.

Then, just as the World Cup was getting under way in South Africa, Rupert Murdoch launched his deal worth $550 million and it was very obvious where a large percentage of this money would be going. No one was under the illusion that the groundsmen mowing the grass at Test venues like Sydney, Auckland and Durban were suddenly going to become millionaires. If I had known that we were on the path to professionalism even in my day, then these events simply confirmed that the fateful decision could hardly be delayed any longer.

CHAPTER FOURTEEN

Professionalism: The Outcome

When the historic announcement to go professional was made in the summer of 1995, the southern hemisphere, due to the examples I have given and many other instances, already had a much greater grasp of what it meant, and how it should be handled, than anyone in the northern hemisphere. They had all but gone professional already in that hemisphere, so when the game was declared open, they just continued further down the path they were already steering.

By utter contrast, there was chaos in the northern hemisphere. Some adopted the bunker mentality, uttering words to the effect that 'Let the southern hemisphere turn pro. We will stay amateur in this part of the world.' Such 'visionaries' were not what the game needed at that time. Then the national unions gave their clubs the opportunity to put the leading players on contracts, which was to turn out to be a major mistake, for it caused concern and uncertainty among the national squads.

The fact was hardly anyone in the northern hemisphere was really prepared for it. That belief has been reinforced time and again in the years that have followed, often to an excruciatingly painful extent. My impression has been that there's been no structure, no overview, no sense of direction coming from those at the top. Still worse, selfish and introspective opinions have meant that the game has been at best in limbo, and at worst in turmoil.

Once rugby went open, it became of greater interest to a lot of outside parties who suddenly felt it might be worthy of a closer look. Some were ruthless businessmen, with no understanding of what the sport had meant and why it was regarded by its participants and followers as so special. That was unfortunate and, in fairness to the administrators, I could see their concern to protect the game from those who sought to use it for their own ends.

However, there was a reluctance to absorb any of these businessmen into the game whatever their background, and this represented a huge missed opportunity in too many cases. By tarring all the investors with the same brush, the sport has squandered the opportunity to bring on board the kind of business and commercial expertise which could have proved highly valuable to the newly professionalised sport. The conflict that did arise between the guardians of the game and the business investors was doubly regrettable, for the piggies in the middle were the players.

Of course, this didn't happen in the southern hemisphere because of Murdoch's scoop in purchasing the TV rights. It was all neat and tidy and tucked away. Also, the structure in the southern hemisphere, with provincial rugby just below the international game, has been an easier product to sell to TV and to handle the transition into professionalism. In the northern hemisphere, we have a completely different culture.

I am the first to agree that the transition to professionalism in this part of the world has been long and laboured. But I still think it was inevitable. The trouble, certainly in England, was that while the RFU were spending twelve months pondering their options, the clubs jumped in and signed up their players. That was the root cause of the problem. Had the two parties come together and worked with one aim, then things would have been very different.

As it is, club rugby has been in such turmoil, especially in England and Wales, that there has been genuine concern that bankruptcy was looming for several clubs. Even before the season 1998–9 had finished, this danger became evident with the difficulties at clubs like London Scottish, Newcastle, Bedford and Richmond. Businessmen like Sir John Hall, who had funded Newcastle, and Ashley Levett, Richmond's principal backer, walked away from the game.

Bristol had bought London Scottish midway through the season to guarantee themselves a Premiership place for the 1999–2000 season, but then in June 1999, London Irish, London Scottish and Richmond came together with the idea of forming one club. Richmond, by then, had all but ceased to exist as a professional club, with the players having drifted off to other employers. It was all a sad, sorry and messy spectacle. But I suspect we have not seen the end of these difficulties. The final result may be even fewer clubs in business by the start of the next century. For some proud clubs which have been in business for well over 100 years, like Richmond who were one of the original founders of the game in England, that is a sad prospect.

It would be absurd to heap all the blame for the difficulties of the club game solely on the unions. After all, certain clubs have made, at the very least, some highly questionable business decisions. Players who were no more than ordinary were paid vastly inflated salaries which no one could sustain or justify. Equally, however, it cannot be denied that discussions with the unions over the future planning of the sport have too often proved frustrating and negative. I put that down to a genuine lack of vision at the top, allied to their fear of the unknown and of losing their position of ascendancy.

While I fully acknowledge that the union has a responsibility to take care of all clubs, whatever their size, it has been my experience that there has existed a lack of judgement and foresight at the highest level of the sport. The cost of that failing has already been bankruptcy for certain clubs.

One mistake I believe the unions have made was mentioned earlier in this book – the number of international matches now being played. The reason is the unions require the income to pay for their huge, new facilities. But there are inherent dangers in this process. The risk of burn-out to players of appearing in fourteen internationals in a single year, as Wales will have played from November 1998 to November 1999, is obvious. Perhaps I'm being unduly pessimistic here – if Wales play only their pool matches in the World Cup, it will be fourteen games. If they went on and reached the final, they would end up playing seventeen or eighteen internationals in under twelve months. Sensible? I don't think so.

The other danger is the risk of overkill in terms of the paying spectator. Throwing the same meal on the table too often might eventually turn the paying customer away. How can there be a sense of occasion to an international if you play once every three or four weeks, on average, for an entire year?

All these matters which have arisen under professionalism, require sensible, calm, properly discussed solutions. But for that to happen, we must have everyone – unions, clubs and players – pulling in the same direction. So far, the complete reverse has been the case. That being so, it is no wonder there has been so much difficulty in the process of integrating professionalism into rugby.

The players have found themselves marooned in the middle of this dispute between club and country. Too little importance has been placed upon the needs of the player, yet he remains of paramount importance. Would Wales be the same without the Quinnells, Jenkins, Howley, Gibbs, Charvis, Howarth, Bateman, Taylor and others? And what would England look like shorn of Johnson, Rodber, Leonard, Bracken, Wilkinson, Guscott, Hill, Back and Dallaglio?

People who do not actually go onto the field of play tend to forget that rugby is such a physically demanding game that the very nature of it makes the player prone to injury. Care must be taken that the load is spread evenly. Therefore, we are surely entitled to ask 'What have the unions in mind?' Do they want to run international squads and play fifteen or sixteen international matches a year? If so, what will happen in the future? Do they expect schoolboys to come through from Under-18s and Under-21s rugby straight into the international side?

I ask because of course at the moment the club system provides that source of recruitment. But the way some unions have been conducting their affairs, one is entitled to ask whether they wish to see the club process shut down and young players groomed for senior international rugby through the respective age-level squads. In other words, players would learn the game by playing for Wales or England Under-16s, Under-18s, Under 21s, Colts and then the A teams before they were ready for the senior side.

If that scenario is indeed in the minds of the unions, then they should be bold enough to admit it. It is certainly a possibility a lot of people have discussed, with youngsters learning the game and developing solely within the confines of the squads through constant training sessions, followed by matches. A whole new generation could grow up without knowing anything about the traditions of club rugby.

If all this sounds wildly futuristic and improbable, then I have bad news for you. It is already reality in New Zealand. There, some of the country's great clubs like Marist and Ponsonby in Auckland, are struggling for survival, partly because they never see any international players wearing their colours these days. The players are contracted to the provinces and the New Zealand international squad; there isn't time or room for anything else in their busy schedules.

That may be all very well for New Zealand, perhaps it suits them, because club rugby was always small in that country compared to provincial and Test levels. However, the clubs still did provide the backbone of their rugby. Some people in New Zealand say this reflects what the public wants to see: top provincial or international games, and not much else.

But what is going to happen ten years down the road in Britain if we end up with a system whereby there is nothing between the very junior clubs playing rugby solely for the fun of it, and the provincial level? Where will our players get competition from then, because I'm sure the provincial concept will not work in this part of the world, because the clubs have always been the founding rock of our game. There is a popular tradition of inter-province games in New Zealand, but not in Britain – and it is always hard to summon up support for a new entity.

For example, Jean Pierre Rives and Jean Claude Skrela were renowned for their play with the great Stade Toulouse club in France; Jo Maso and, a little later, Didier Codorniou, those delightful dancing French centres, played superbly for Narbonne. In Wales, clubs such as Cardiff, Swansea, Newport, Neath and Llanelli have contributed countless players to the Welsh international team; so, too, in England where the likes of David Duckham, Fran Cotton, Peter Rossborough, Peter Preece and Geoff Evans all played for the powerful Coventry club. More recently, look at Bath's contribution to England sides and now Leicester's. There is scant evidence of widespread support for the concept of East Wales or West of England. It simply isn't something that would work over here, in my view. It never has.

However, is it now the wish of some administrators that we overthrow our system and ape the southern hemisphere? I ask these questions because, if you accept, as one surely must, that the club system provides the development programme, why do some unions such as the Welsh Rugby Union and the Scottish Rugby Union seem so negative about creating a strong club system? Why keep putting off the formation of a new structure to match the requirements of the new game? I, like many other people in Wales, await with interest the further steps which may yet be taken in the coming months and years as professional rugby continues to evolve. For example, will a British League, which seemed near to reality at one stage in late 1998 and early 1999, continue to be discussed, and eventually emerge?

And how will the great conundrum concerning the players and the need to protect them from burnout, finally be resolved?

If you have a player performing in this highly physical sport for ten or eleven months of the year, then you are shortening his career, perhaps by years. It is just not possible to play high-pressure club rugby all winter, with internationals dotted throughout that programme, and then go off on tour in the so-called off-season and play more. You will end up wrecked by rugby after a few years.

What is needed is not more rugby, as the authorities seem to believe, but higher quality rugby played less often. Time for recovery from the physical exertions of playing at the top level, is of paramount importance. Remember, resting is training, and players must have a break from this immensely tough physical game they now play.

What we are all looking for is a structured season which gives us a meaningful fixture list. I would like to see that based on a cross-border competition, a British League, but whether that will happen I am not sure. Compromise has to be reached between clubs and unions.

What I am sure of is that our leading players, people like Rob Howley of Cardiff and Wales, must be protected from the rigours of playing too much rugby. I believe the top men should play a maximum of 36 matches in a season and I would formulate that on the following basis: 22 league games, hopefully in a British League, eight internationals and six European games. There has to be an element of flexibility built into that equation – for example, if a leading side gets into the last four or even the final of the European competition, then of course the best players are going to be wanted for those games.

I do not believe there should be any restriction on a player representing his country. That should be paramount. But the national unions, like the clubs, have to be realistic. It makes no sense for a player to be asked to appear in fourteen internationals in a single year. For a start, the unions must understand clubs simply have to survive. However, on the club side, it is not fair to expect a top player to appear in forty club games alone in a single season.

Sharing the load is vital. That means a close liaison between unions and clubs to sort out the ideal structure. A less selfish approach on both sides is what is required. You cannot allow a situation to go on whereby a top player such as Martin Johnson of Leicester and England, plays fifty-four matches in one season, as happened a year or so back. That is simply unacceptable in so physical a sport, especially as they are all competitive matches now, with cups and league positions at stake.

This is a very demanding game these days. You need not only to be in good shape physically but also mentally. It's true that in our day, there were plenty of fixtures and the rugby was tough. In the first two months of a season, Cardiff might play twenty matches. It was Wednesday, Saturday, Wednesday, Saturday and you would be meeting the likes of Swansea, Llanelli and Neath. No easy games there!

Then you had Barbarians fixtures and appearances for Wales. You would be touching thirty appearances at home and then, when you went on tour, maybe another fifteen games there. Someone like Dai Morris of Wales would play as many as sixty games in a season. But that was too much. And today, it is even tougher a sport so players should play much, much less. Players need peaks and troughs, they need to look carefully at what they're aiming for. You cannot keep on in top gear especially if you have injuries.

Some will claim that satisfying both club and country is simply not possible, but I don't accept that. More negotiations need to take place between all parties concerned before we can say we have reached the definitive solution. But if compromise is a trait both sides bring to their discussions, then there is no earthly reason to suppose a satisfactory conclusion is out of reach. What has made an answer so difficult to find so far has been the intransigence of certain people in power within the game. The long dispute between Cardiff and Swansea with the Welsh Rugby Union has been a classic example.

Those in official circles tend to repeat a familiar line when questioned about their feelings towards the club owners. 'They want to take over the whole game' is their cry. Well, I, for one, do not accept that. I know Peter Thomas extremely well, the man who has put so much time and effort into the Cardiff club, and I can say with my hand on heart that I know he has no such agenda. He is a businessman and he makes no secret of the fact that he believes in the Cardiff club and believes in rugby and its future under professionalism. Of course, he is seeking an eventual return on his money – who wouldn't in any business venture? There hasn't been the slightest sign of that return as yet, and it may be a long while before there is. But in the meantime, Peter continues to provide financial support for one of the greatest clubs in Welsh or British rugby. Yet still he is villified in some circles for providing that backing, and for the life of me I cannot understand why.

Peter Thomas doesn't want to own the Welsh Rugby Union, he doesn't want to deny players like Robert Howley, the Cardiff scrum-half, the opportunity to go and play for and, in Howley's case, captain his country. The idea that Thomas would want to prevent that is laughable. Yet still these disingenuous ideas are put about as Thomas's views. It is appalling.

What people like Peter Thomas say, if anyone cares to listen, and others in England such as Nigel Wray of Saracens and Tom Walkinshaw of Gloucester, is that if they are bankrolling some of their countries' leading clubs, and therefore providing the training ground for present and future England players, surely they are entitled to have more of a say when it comes to decisions that affect their club and their financial situation. They aren't saying, get rid of the Welsh Rugby Union, sack the RFU at Twickenham – we will run rugby. That is untrue, a belief put about by those whom it suited to spread such mis-information.

They simply want their voice to be heard, their views to be taken into consideration when a decision is made. I see nothing wrong in that. For the unions to tell clubs they cannot negotiate with sponsors who have expressed an interest in supporting Bath, Saracens or Cardiff if they are playing in Europe is baffling. The unions want to do it themselves, yet where in the business world – and remember, rugby is now a business whether we like it or not – does a company's board of management have to allow an outside body to make decisions on its behalf?

It is not my impression that every one of those who sit on each country's official governing body, whether it be the WRU, the RFU, the SRU or the IRFU, believes it necessary to frustrate and impede their clubs' natural progress in a business environment, in this way. That cannot be true. But the voices of a few have prevented what ought to have been significant steps being taken by the clubs to embrace professionalism through the striking of their own deals, and being trusted to do so. That, surely, is the natural way, leaving the governing bodies to run international rugby and administer the many junior clubs who continue to need their support. For professionalism is not for everyone in the game, that much is already plainly apparent.

What is needed, what the game is crying out for in this part of the world, is mutual trust so that people know where everybody is coming from and there are no hidden agendas. We need responsibility for certain aspects affecting the leading professional clubs to be devolved, but with the unions always there for advice and help if required. They, after all, are the guardians of the game and should remain so.

None of this enters the realms of rocket science. It seems to me it ought to be a simple process to allow the clubs a voice, to let them negotiate the commercial deals that affect them primarily and, in return, to expect an approach, an attitude and an understanding which is in sympathy with this game and its great traditions and ways. Should we ever arrive at that state, then I believe we can say we have at last adapted properly and professionally to this open game which arrived in our midst in such haste and has caused such difficulty and concern in the months and years that have followed.

Index